CONTENTS

NOTES
For convenience, ease-of-growing symbols
have been incorporated in the A-Z sections.
They can be interpreted as follows:
*   * Easy to grow plants
  * * Plants which require more than average care
* * * Temperamental or difficult to grow plants

Published in 1987 by Octopus Books Ltd,
59 Grosvenor Street, London W1

© Cathay Books 1983
ISBN 0 7064 2589 8

Printed in Hong Kong

INTRODUCTION

Patios, windowboxes and other containers offer an exciting extension to traditional gardening, especially for those with little garden space. Even the tiniest back garden can be turned into an attractive patio with a variety of plants. An empty balcony or a plain front porch can be transformed into a blaze of colour with hanging baskets, urns and tubs of contrasting flowering plants. Patios, of course, are not restricted to confined space gardens. An 'outdoor living area' is always appreciated in a large garden.

Windowboxes are the perfect way to brighten up the exterior of homes which have no garden. All town houses and flats have windows and that usually means window-ledges suitable for anchoring windowboxes to. There are various containers to suit all types of dwellings – from simple white plastic window-boxes for modern homes, to ornate terracotta containers for older properties. Better still, you can make your own wooden windowboxes to fit the available space – much cheaper and not difficult.

One of the main advantages of container gardening is the flexibility it offers. Special soil and moisture conditions can be provided in tubs, windowboxes and hanging baskets – extending the range of plants that can be grown. Colourful displays can be maintained all-year-round by replanting containers when the contents have passed their best. Winter boxes, filled with evergreens, can be under-planted with dwarf flowering bulbs to provide colour through the spring. The choice of plants to replace these for a summer display is endless, but fuchsias, pansies and impatiens are always popular.

Although most container and patio plants are purely decorative, there are some exceptions. Herbs, of course, are traditionally grown. They are especially useful – either in a windowbox or in tubs just outside the back door – within easy reach of the kitchen. A raised herb bed on the patio also looks most attractive and has a wonderful aroma! A surprising range of fruit and vegetables can also be grown. Strawberries, cucumbers and tomatoes are suitable container plants; small fruit trees and soft fruit bushes can be planted directly into the soil on the patio.

A patio – large or small – adds a new dimension to outdoor living by extending the time normally spent in the garden. At different times it can be a place for entertaining, relaxing, for the children to play in, or a quiet spot to work in. A patio adjacent to the house can be treated as an additional room in summer, and furnished accordingly – with table and chairs. On a warm summer's evening, nothing is more enjoyable than a barbecue on the patio.

For the gardener with an eye for design, a patio offers plenty of scope. All sorts of containers can be used, from wooden hanging baskets and windowboxes to terracotta jars, stone troughs and wooden half-barrels. In addition, there are usually opportunities for planting some material directly into the soil. Small flowerbeds between paving stones are most effective.

Few patio sites are perfect. By virtue of its position the patio may have to house the dustbin, an oil tank or ugly drain pipes, for example. But these unsightly objects can be hidden by positioning trees, raised beds or screens carefully, and climbers can make any wall or screen look attractive. The potential growing space on the walls of a small patio is often greater than the ground area and should never be wasted. Apart from the flowering climbers, such as clematis, cotoneasters and honeysuckles, many of the dwarf fruit trees can be fan-trained to splendid effect against a wall.

One of the most appealing aspects of patio and windowbox gardening is the comparatively small amount of effort required to create an attractive display. No strenuous digging, constant weeding or laborious mowing is involved. The key to success is careful planning – selecting suitable plants and positioning them for maximum effect. The chart on pages 74-77 provides at-a-glance information on growing requirements of patio and windowbox plants – especially useful when choosing plants to be grouped together. The A-Z section tells you how to look after each one.

CONTAINERS

WINDOWBOXES

A well-stocked windowbox can bring character to even the most ordinary house, or brighten the dreary facade of an office block in town. For the flat dweller without a garden, window-boxes are invaluable. With a little thought they can provide pleasure all year round. The choice of plants can vary with your likes and needs. In spring a colourful display can be created with bulbs planted the previous autumn – hyacinths, polyanthus, narcissi, low-growing tulips and dwarf irises all provide possibilities. These can then be changed for colourful summer bedding plants, such as pansies, fuchsias and stocks. A herb box is ideal for the kitchen window.

Windowboxes can be fitted to most windows – obviously taking great care that they are securely fixed to prevent them falling or sliding off. Most sash windows will take a box actually sitting on the sill, but casement windows that swing open have to have the box slung below the sill, and the plants must be low enough to allow the window clearance above them.

When fixing, remember that windowboxes are very heavy when filled with moist soil and plants. Be careful to check that all brackets and fixing screws are adequate for the job. If you are hanging a trough below a windowsill, make sure that the trough is strong enough to take the stress of being supported by a bracket at each end, otherwise the bottom might drop out together with the contents. The dimensions of the windowbox will obviously depend on the size of windowsill, but it should have a depth of 15-20 cm (6-8 inches) to give a good root-run for most plants. If the window is particularly wide it is better to have several short boxes rather than one long one as smaller boxes are more robust and rigid, and easier to handle.

The timber used for a windowbox should be at least 2.5 cm (1 inch) thick for the structure of the box. If you are using plywood make sure you use exterior or marine ply as this will withstand the weather and dampness. All nails and screws should be rust-proof and the glue should be waterproof. Treat timber with a wood preservative that will not affect plant life –

most manufacturers produce one that is formulated for this purpose. Some of the copper-based preservatives may leave the wood with a green tinge, but this can be painted over. If you prefer not to paint the outside of the window-box, choose one that will leave the wood with a more natural colour.

All windowboxes should have adequate drainage in the base to allow excess water to drain away. If the box is hung below the sill, be sure that the holes are placed so that the water will not run down the wall and leave an unsightly stain. The holes should be placed near the front edge so that any drips fall free of the wall. When positioning the windowbox on the sill, place a removable drip tray underneath it to collect any excess water. As most sills slope to stop water standing on them, wedges should be placed under the windowboxes to keep them level and lift them clear of the ledge. This helps with drainage and aeration.

Some gardeners prefer to keep all their plants in individual pots and sink these into a peat,

A composite windowbox provides a colourful spring display – primulas, hyacinths, crocus and a dwarf juniper are an effective combination.

Practical Gardeners' Guides

THE PATIO & WINDOWBOX GARDEN

David Papworth

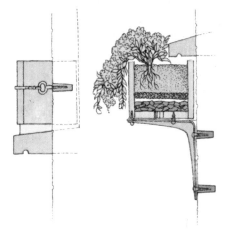

Iris, fuchsias and yellow alyssum – plants of different heights are combined to provide an attractive summer windowbox.

LEFT: *Above the sill, secure boxes with wall plugs and galvanised wire. Use a wedge to keep the box level.*
RIGHT: *Brackets, rustproof screws and wall plugs will hold a windowbox firmly beneath the sill.*

Plants can be potted individually and then inserted into a windowbox filled with peat or vermiculite. This makes transplanting and maintenance of individual plants easier.

vermiculite or perlite bed in the windowbox rather than planting directly into the box. This has the advantage that an ailing plant can be removed without disturbing the roots of the others. If the tops of the pots are filled with the same materials as the windowbox the pots become almost invisible. As an alternative, a board with holes, into which the pots can be dropped, can be fixed to the wall with brackets. If planted with trailing specimens the pots are concealed by the foliage.

By careful selection of plants, windowboxes can provide attractive all-year-round displays. For a colourful springtime show plant bulbs – daffodils, crocus and tulips – and interplant with evergreens. For a summer display, plant in May and choose from petunias, impatiens (busy Lizzie), asters, heliotropes, helianthe-mums and mesembryanthemums. Alterna-tively, opt for begonias, salvias and pansies which will flower all through summer and early autumn – until the first frosts appear.

Maintain windowboxes through the winter months by planting with evergreens; winter-flowering erica is a good choice. Some of the summer-flowering plants, such as santolina, offer attractive foliage in winter.

Pelargoniums (geraniums) are amongst the most popular windowbox plants because of their long flowering period. If you want flowers for cutting – to enhance the inside of your home as well as the outside – choose anemones, dahlias, tulips and iris. For fragrance, consider alyssums, antirrhinums and violas.

Composite arrangements can be most effec-tive in windowboxes – providing contrast in shape, size and colour. For best results, make sure that the plants you group together can easily be grown in the same compost or soil, at the same temperature and in the same light situation. For example, wall-flowers, pansies and violas can be grown together in a lime-containing soil. Use the chart on pages 74-77 as a quick guide to plants which flourish under similar conditions.

HANGING BASKETS

Hanging baskets can brighten up plain walls, porches, doorways, basement areas, pergolas and archways, and they can bring colour and interest up off the ground to eye level or above. There are free-hanging baskets or half baskets to fit on to walls. They are made from wire, plastic, wood, or pottery. The wire models can be painted, galvanized, or dipped into plastic to make them weatherproof, while the plastic variety can be supplied with or without an integral reservoir for water.

Again the planted baskets can be quite heavy, so great care must be taken to check that the supporting brackets or hooks and chains are strong enough and firmly fixed to the wall. It is possible to obtain supporting hooks that allow the basket to be raised and lowered for watering and maintenance. This is particularly valuable where it would be difficult to water from a window above.

It is vital to provide a good heart to the basket to supply water and food for the roots of the plants. First line the basket with sphagnum moss or osmunda fibre, then fill it to within 4-5 cm (1½-2 inches) of the rim with a mixture of peat, to absorb moisture, and a suitable com-post (see page 24). It is possible to use a plastic sheet in place of the moss to keep the moisture from evaporating too quickly, but as this can look unsightly it is best to place the plastic sheet between the peat and an outer lining of moss, so that the plastic is hidden. To prevent the

A cross section of a wire basket showing the centre core of moss peat, surrounded by peat-based compost. An outer layer of moss hides the plastic sheet lining. Small plants can be introduced through the sides of the basket.

The minimum of effort is required to grow flowering plants, such as these calceolarias and fuchsias, in a plastic hanging basket which has an integral reservoir of water in the base of the container.

moss then appearing dry, spray occasionally with water. If plastic sheeting is used, it must be pierced with holes for drainage. 'Foam' basket liners are also available.

The sides of hanging baskets can be planted as well as the top surface, provided this is done as the basket is being filled. Once the base of the basket has been lined with moss and the plastic sheet, some trailing plants can be inserted through the mesh, moss and plastic and their roots spread out and packed round with the peat mixture. Continue this procedure, gradually filling up the basket and completing it with the top planting.

When finished, the basket should be immersed in a container of water and allowed to soak for a couple of hours. Allow the basket to drain before hanging it in its final position. Flourishing baskets require regular watering, preferably by immersing the whole basket in a bucket of water about once a day, although this can be difficult if you have prolific trailing plants. Hanging baskets should also be fed at least weekly from July through to the frosts for the best results.

Suitable plants for hanging baskets include anemones, begonias (tuberous-rooted), campanulas, fuchsias, lobelias and pelargoniums. During the winter months baskets can be planted with suitable subjects such as dwarf junipers surrounded with hardy succulents, and small evergreen climbers, such as small-leaved ivies. If you use these as temporary

An easy way to water plants in a hanging basket is to immerse the entire basket in a box lined with plastic sheeting, and filled with water. The basket can be left to soak for a few hours.

9

fillers, keep them in pots rather than uproot them each time. Choose varieties that have varied leaf form and colour. Alternatively 'winter baskets' can be moved to the north side of the house and other baskets planted with spring-flowering plants and bulbs can be hung; these in turn can be replaced with summer-flowering baskets so that you have a colourful display throughout the year.

There are plenty of flowers that thrive in hanging baskets. The more exotic ones are tender and can only be used in the summer; they need the protection of a greenhouse or conservatory during the winter. There are other plants that can grow in baskets: for the gourmet, a basketful of strawberries grows very well, safe from the harmful attentions of slugs and other ground-based pests. Another basket planted with mint, chives and parsley can serve the cook, particularly if it is within easy reach of the kitchen window.

It is easy to be carried away with enthusiasm and overdo the number of plants squeezed into a hanging basket, but try to avoid this. It is better to keep to a simple colour scheme or to have a basic planting with variations in the flower colour. A basket full of one kind of plant, such as petunias, can provide a marvellous spectacle while a complicated planting can end up looking a mess.

TUBS AND URNS

Tubs and urns are the most common of the containers used for planting and can be used for a variety of purposes from brightening up a dull patch in the garden to adorning balconies, terraces or patios, or even decorating a doorway or a flight of steps. They are particularly useful for giving height to what would otherwise be a rather flat area.

Tubs fall into two categories – the round half-barrel and the Versailles square tub. The latter has a removable side so that maintenance of the soil and root pruning can be undertaken without lifting the plant out of the tub. Normally both kinds are made from wood, but you can now get plastic and glass-fibre tubs too. The advantage with these new types is that they do not rot. However, the cheaper models are not particularly rigid and can become distorted into strange shapes by the weight of the soil. The ideal choice is a tub made from hardwood that

A cross section of a large wooden tub showing (from top to bottom) the layers of pebbles, potting compost, peat, capillary matting and crocks.

has been pressure treated with preservative as this will last for many years.

Urns are usually constructed from stone, lead, or re-constituted stone. The latter is crushed stone that is mixed with cement and pressed into a mould to produce a replica urn with all the looks of the original stone but at a fraction of the cost.

Some tubs and urns are constructed without drainage holes, in which case sufficient holes must be bored before the container is used. This is a relatively easy task if the containers are made of timber and plastic, but if they are made of stone there is always the possibility of breaking or chipping the edge. It is wise to use a power drill and a small masonry bit to drill a guide hole right through the base of the container; then use a larger masonry bit – as large as your drill will take – and drill halfway from the inside and then complete the hole from the outside. In this way it is possible to avoid chipping the edges.

If a wooden tub is used it is advisable to lift it clear of the ground by positioning it on a few bricks. This allows air to pass freely underneath, keeping the timber dry to prevent rotting. It also makes the tub a less attractive proposition for unwanted insects.

A layer of crocks (broken clay pots) or stones should be spread over the base of the container, making sure that the drainage holes are not blocked. The depth of the crocks depends on the size of the tub or urn, but as a general rule you should allow not less than 25 cm (10 inches) above the crocks for soil, unless you are growing alpines or plants with very shallow roots. Spread a piece of capillary matting over the crocks. This will allow any surplus water to drain away but prevent the soil from seeping down and silting up the drainage holes. On top of the matting put a 5 cm (2 inch) layer of peat and then place the soil mixture on top of this. Use a potting compost with either a soil or peat base.

One of the advantages of containers is that they can be moved to a new site if required.

Once a tub or urn has been planted, however, moving such a weight can be quite a problem. One way to overcome this is to mount the containers on trolleys or castors and, provided the surface is fairly smooth, the container can then be trundled around without strain.

The siting of the containers needs to be considered carefully. Avoid placing them in cold and windy corners, otherwise the plants will be stunted. On the other hand a sheltered and warm arbour will encourage tender plants to thrive.

Should you wish to grow plants that will not normally flourish in the type of soil in your area – such as camellias in an alkaline or chalky soil – a container can provide the answer as it can be filled with a soil mixture that suits the individual plant's requirements.

RIGHT: Climbing plants, such as sweet peas, can be trained up a wig-wam of canes in a tub for a tall arrangement.

FAR RIGHT: A Versailles tub is an effective container for a clipped bay tree.

ABOVE: A small peach tree can be grown successfully in a half-barrel. An underplanting of helianthemums enhances the display.

FROM LEFT TO RIGHT
– A barrel cut lengthways is the
perfect place to grow your
favourite herbs.
– A tall chimney pot provides an
ideal stand for a potted cistus.
– For a rustic look, cover a
wooden box with lengths of split
larch poles and fill with flowering
plants, such as pelargoniums,
lobelias and alyssum.
– An old kitchen sink can be
turned into an attractive
container by covering with a peat,
sand and cement mixture.
– A simple wire frame can be fixed
in a container to enable climbing
plants, such as clematis, to be
grown.

UNUSUAL CONTAINERS

Apart from the variety of tubs and urns available in garden centres there are many other sources for attractive and interesting containers that can make an individual contribution to your patio area. Drums, barrels, boxes, old pipes, sinks, baths, chimney pots, buckets, jars, washtubs – in fact almost anything that has been used as a container and is weatherproof is a potential holder for plants.

Before using any container that might have held a toxic substance, it must be washed out thoroughly. Timber that has been creosoted must be allowed to weather to neutralize the chemicals that will kill plant life. Plastic drums that have held corrosive substances may have to be treated chemically to make the container harmless. You will need to consult someone with a knowledge of the chemistry involved. Some metals can corrode and develop poisonous salts, and may need coating with protective paint or lining with plastic sheeting to isolate the plants from the metal; again you will need expert advice.

Often the container has to be cut, either in half or to have one end opened. Before doing this consider if it is the best way of using the receptacle. It may be possible to make two interesting plant holders by cutting halfway down the container rather than across. In this way you can get shapes that stack to give an attractive vertical arrangement. Such containers should be reinforced to strengthen the cut edges so that they do not collapse when filled with soil.

Pre-planted flower pots can look charming when placed in the end of old chimney pots and pipes and can easily be lifted out when the plants fade, to be replaced with fresh ones. The height of many chimney pots and pipes makes them vulnerable to being knocked over, so weight the bases to make them more stable.

Wooden boxes should be treated against rot and insect attack, and if they are on the flimsy side they can be reinforced by fixing additional timber on the outside. This can be made into a decorative feature if split larch poles with the bark still intact are used; or tongued and grooved timber, such as cedar, attached. The larch wood gives a rustic finish while the cedar can be treated or varnished to give a more sophisticated look.

Metal boxes should be treated on the inside with a bitumen paint, and provided with adequate drainage holes. The exterior can be left if the finish is weatherproof, but if it is likely to rust to produce unsightly oxides then the metal should be protected; again you can use a bitumen paint if it is a ferrous metal, but use a lacquer on cleaned copper. When in doubt about the effect of the metal on plant life it is best to play safe and line the container with a plastic sheet to keep the soil away from the metal. Remember to pierce holes in the bottom of the sheet so that surplus water can drain through the holes in the metal.

Sinks and baths make excellent containers. The old-fashioned stone sinks are rare and in great demand, but modern white-glazed sinks are more common and can be disguised by painting a layer of PVA glue over the exterior and then spreading on a mixture of 2 parts peat, 1 part cement and 1 part sharp sand. This should be mixed with water and 50 ml (2½ fl oz) of PVA adhesive for each sink to make a thick, rough composition. The mixture is then spread over the outside of the sink to give an attractive rough, stone-like texture. When dry the sink can be filled with soil and planted.

Baths can be left unadorned if they are ancient and of interesting shape with fancy claw feet, but modern baths look best if they have a brick or stone wall built around them to form a raised bed.

Pipes come in a variety of widths and lengths and even pre-cast concrete drainage pipes that come in sections can be used as containers, although they should be regarded as permanent as they lack a base. The smaller ones of pottery, plastic, metal and concrete can be very useful for adding height and variety to the patio. Long pieces of pipe need to be filled to a good depth with crocks. For lightness, pieces of expanded polystyrene can be wedged in the pipes to allow for good drainage.

Whichever type of container is chosen, half the battle is positioning it correctly. Try the empty container in several places to make sure that you are happy with it. It is a good idea to place it on a join in the paving so that drainage water can seep away without leaving unsightly marks on the paving itself. Once you have decided on the best position the container can then be filled with soil and suitable plants.

13

PATIOS

WHERE TO SITE A PATIO

Patio was originally the Spanish word for an interior courtyard, but it is commonly used in this country to refer to a paved area adjoining the house for relaxing and entertaining. For most people a patio provides a convenient place to sit in the sun on every available opportunity, and, by careful positioning and screening, it is possible to keep the temperatures up and so extend the period of outdoor living. For the few days when clear blue skies in the summer make the heat rise, some shading is important, and this should be considered when looking at sites. Taking advantage of the shade offered by an already established tree is one idea for this.

A south-facing position is obviously the ideal choice for a patio, but if this is not possible choose a site that makes the most of the morning or evening sun. Consider what the patio will be used for – will it be for entertaining in the evening, or will you be needing a small private sun patch in the morning. Check that neighbouring trees and buildings do not cast shadows across the patio when you are most likely to want to use it, and that the area is not overlooked by a neighbour's window. Privacy is an important consideration and a shift of a few feet in siting your patio could make all the difference. It is vital to consider all these points carefully, for once the patio has been constructed and planted it is very expensive to move to another site.

When you have decided on the site, determine the shape and size you would like it to be. Peg out the area with canes and string so that you can see just how big it is going to be, and how it relates to the rest of the garden and the house. An alteration at this stage is easy and costs only a few moments of your time. When it is pegged out, place a chair within the area and sit there to make sure that it is right for the sun, and that shelter from the wind is provided. Consider whether you will need some cover from rain, protection for your garden furniture, and storage space for all those other indispensable items that make for relaxing in the sun.

It seems a contradiction to find a sunny site and then build a shady structure to keep the sun off, but if the design is right it should keep the sun off you when it is high in the sky, but allows it to shine underneath the canopy when it is lower, in the spring, autumn and winter. As an alternative consider a pergola and clothe it with plants that conveniently lose their leaves when the sun is needed and grow a filter of fresh ones when shade is required.

TYPES OF PATIOS AND USES

Patios can be rooms which have an open wall, or walls without a ceiling; they can be courtyards, terraces, or areas for relaxing, dining or other activities. The one thing that these all have in common is the floor, which is the most crucial part of any patio.

The material for the floor should have a smooth, even surface; this will prevent chairs 'rocking', and it will be easy to sweep clean and maintain. It should also have an attractive colour and texture. Choose a material that will not reflect the glare from the sun, that dries out reasonably quickly after the rain, and that has a non-slip surface.

Paving slabs are usually the first material to

Even the smallest area by the side of the house can be paved and used to enjoy the sun. Shade is provided by dwarf trees.

14

A larger patio offers more scope. A vine-covered pergola provides shelter for a barbecue, table and chairs. The fountain makes an attractive focal point.

The patio need not be adjacent to the house. A site at the end of the garden may make the most of sunny days – away from the shade of the house.

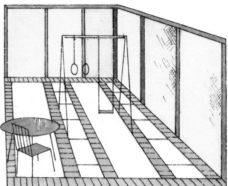

Break up a large expanse of paving by planting areas with trees and decorative grasses. Filling in areas with gravel also looks effective – and makes the paving stones go further.

Add interest to a large patio floorspace by laying concrete slabs and paving with a brick surround. A lightweight screen around the sides provides some protection and privacy.

spring to mind. They are easily obtained and laid, require little maintenance, and are fairly easy on the pocket. However a large paved area can look monotonous and needs to be broken up visually.

Other materials include: real York stone slabs (but these cost a small fortune); bricks, which can look very interesting if laid in patterns, but they need to be a hard, frost-resistant variety; tar-macadam, which will give a smooth surface but will become soft in really hot weather; gravel, which is cheap but uncomfortable to walk or lie on; sand, which is unstable and dusty but is rather like having your own beach; wood, which is very pleasant but needs to be installed properly and requires some maintenance; concrete, which has to be laid well with other materials otherwise it will look like a section of motorway; and tiles. A combination of surfaces is probably best on the eye, and the pocket. A large patio area will not dominate the garden if it is broken up visually with changes in colour and texture, but bear in mind how the plants will look against the various shades.

For entertaining, space should be provided for food and drink. A barbecue will provide a pleasing focal point but remember that a permanent structure takes up space while a mobile model can be brought out onto the patio just on the occasions when you need it.

Whether you have benches or tables and chairs depends on the style of eating and drinking that you want to provide – a formal dinner table can only cater for a chosen few, while the stand-up informal buffet can accommodate a whole crowd of people.

Depending on the proposed uses of the patio, various forms of screen wall can be considered. There are pierced concrete blocks that can be used to form a decorative wall; bricks, timber or open structures that can be covered by climbing plants. Some screen walls will need to be substantial as they have to take weight as well as the buffeting of the weather, others can be lighter if they have nothing to support and are only decorative in a sheltered corner. If positioned correctly, a screen can provide shelter from cool winds and give the patio more privacy. Overhead beams should be strong enough to support themselves as well as growing plants and supporting blinds if needed.

Permanent structures should really be made to last as long as the house. If in doubt about brick constructions and planning permission for a large undertaking, have a word with the local planning officer at the council offices. He will advise you on what you are allowed to erect and where, but for most paved areas and simple garden structures no permission is required.

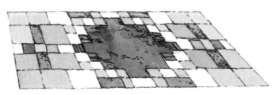

Different coloured paving stones can be combined to brighten up a square or rectangular patio. Formal and informal designs are both effective.

An attractive circular patio can be constructed with bricks or tiles. The area is screened by a low hedge and a timber frame for climbers.

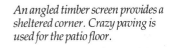

An angled timber screen provides a sheltered corner. Crazy paving is used for the patio floor.

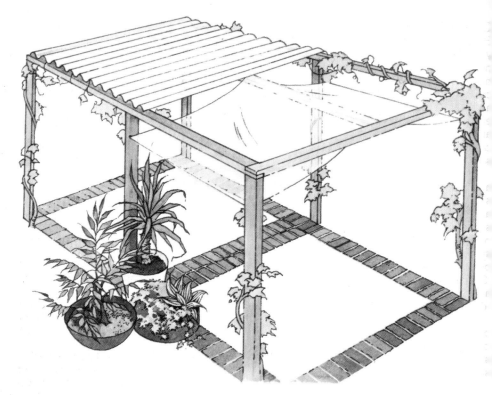

PATIO DESIGN

If you are lucky enough to have lots of space you can design the patio area on a grand scale, using large paving slabs and creating areas for different functions. If, like most of us, you only have limited space and budget it takes a degree of ingenuity to make a worthwhile patio. Use moderately sized furnishings, small-scale building units, a brick or sett floor, raised planting to give height, and make the most of wall and overhead plants to create a sense of space.

Often it helps to make the patio look as if it is an extension to a room. Use similar materials, and keep the patio screens or walls the same proportions as the internal walls. This adds another living space to the house.

Patios can be square, rectangular, circular or free-form – the shape is immaterial provided the patio is functional and is in keeping with the rest of the garden and house style. Many patios are just a paved area that could be improved with some screening to add height, shelter and privacy, or simply extra plants.

Overhead screens keep out the rain – especially useful where the patio is used as a play area; corrugated plastic is ideal.

One idea is to make a list of the needs of your family when designing the patio area so that all possible requirements are considered. For instance children need a dry area on which to play on damp days, the elderly require a snug corner out of draughts and a short distance from shelter in case of rain. Families with young children may want an area to leave a baby safely. . . and adults need somewhere to relax after work.

By gradually working through these various demands and the natural limitations of the site, the shape of the patio will evolve. Walls, screens, overhead beams, blinds, planting, benches and decorative features such as pools, raised beds and built-in barbecues will all start filling in areas on or next to the patio. When the layout is complete, tidy up the whole design so that all the lines and shapes are pleasing to the eye as well as functional.

CONSTRUCTION

Having prepared the layout for the patio design you will want to know how to construct it. You need to be sure that when it rains the patio will not subside, or hold water, that frost will not crack the surface, walls will remain standing, and that a long life of trouble-free pleasure is ensured. By following time-tested practices and rules you should have a patio on which you can relax sure in the knowledge that there is a secure structure around you.

Areas to be paved need to have a firm foundation so that the paving stones will not crack or sink. Mark out the area for paving with pegs and string before excavating. Dig out the top soil to a depth of about 18 cm (7 inches) and remove to a safe place as it is invaluable for spreading over the rest of the garden. Level the bottom of the excavation and spread a 7.5 cm (3 inch) layer of hardcore or rubble over the area and compact well with a hand-rammer to form a firm base.

Over the hardcore, place 5 cm (2 inches) of builders' sand to fill in any gaps, then lay the paving on top of this, ensuring that the top surface of the paving is the same level as the surrounding ground.

If the paving needs to withstand some traffic of wheelbarrows, garden equipment, and plant containers, apply five spots of mortar to each 60 cm (2 feet) square paving slab. Smaller slabs and bricks should be laid on a 2.5 cm (1 inch) bed of mortar laid on top of the sand and tapped well down with a wooden mallet to form a firm and level surface. The surface itself should have a fall or slope towards the outer edge, away from the house to allow rain to run off freely. The slope should be at the rate of 5 cm (2 inches) for every 3 metres (10 feet). Where there is no suitable edge for the rain to run off, build a drain and soakaway in the centre and have the paving sloping towards the drain.

If you use gravel or sand as a patio surface the main problem is keeping the area weed-free. If you use capillary matting over a 7.5 cm (3 inch) layer of hardcore to prevent the sand or gravel being washed into the hardcore, a 7.5 cm (3 inch) layer of sand or gravel should keep deep-rooted weeds at bay. The annuals can be held in check by dosing the area with a long-lasting weedkiller. Of course the matting is not essential and a persistent weed killer will take care of any weeds if applied annually.

Timber used out of doors should be treated against rot and insect attack. Ensure that where it will be in close proximity to plants the pre-

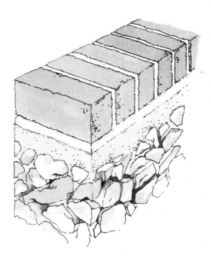

A cross section through a patio floor showing the lower layer of hardcore, the narrow layer of sand with the paving laid on top.

If bricks are used as the patio surface, they must be laid on a 2.5 cm (1 inch) bed of mortar on top of the sand and hardcore.

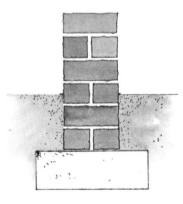

Where the patio has brick walls, foundations are necessary to distribute the weight of the wall and make it more stable. The concrete foundation should be twice the width of the wall and at least 15 cm (6 inches) beneath the soil.

servative is safe for them. The timber should be raised off the ground to allow air to flow underneath, keeping it dry. The most satisfactory method is to build concrete or brick piers on which the timber can rest. Always use rust-free nails and screws and be sure that the top surface of the timber is smooth and free from splinters, splits, or rough edges.

Where there is a large expanse of plain paving the gaps between the slabs can be left open and free from mortar. These crevices can then be filled with potting compost and planted with low creeping plants, such as thyme, to soften the look of the area.

If the patio design requires walls of brick, stone or blocks, it is important to have good foundations to spread the weight of the wall over a larger area so that it will not crack or lean. Most manufacturers of pre-cast blocks give recommended dimensions for foundations but as a general rule make the concrete strip twice the width of the wall and at least 15 cm (6 inches) thick. It should be 15 cm (6 inches) below the soil surface, more if the soil has been disturbed or built up.

Timber screens and beams should be fixed securely and be strong enough to support not only their own weight but also the weight of any plants that they are going to support. All fixings should be rust-proof and where adhesive is used, make sure that it is waterproof.

PLANTS ON THE PATIO

Large containers, such as tubs and urns, always look attractive on patios. Most types of patio also offer the opportunity of planting some material directly into the soil. Shrubs and small trees are suitable for direct planting and many of them thrive in even the poorest soil. *Betula pendula* is particularly tolerant of difficult soil. Rhododendrons and fruit bushes can be used to break up large paved areas, and climbing plants, such as grape vines, are most effective against a screen or wall.

If the soil on the patio is poor, it should be removed to a depth of at least 15 cm (6 inches). Check that drainage is adequate by pouring one or two buckets of water into the hole. If the water does not drain satisfactorily, break up the sub-soil by digging it thoroughly. Finally, replace the top soil with fresh, fertile soil or compost.

If there isn't an area readily available for direct planting it is usually possible to create one – simply by removing a few paving stones. Raised beds are another alternative. These are normally composed of stone, or paving stones held together with hardcore or concrete. They offer the opportunity of growing plants at waist height – particularly advantageous for fragrant herbs and flowers.

A POOL ON THE PATIO

One of the great joys of a patio is to be able to sit in the sunshine and listen to the sounds of nature. Water gives this pleasure an added dimension whether it is just the gentle drip of water, the gurgle of a waterfall, or the splash of a fountain. Visually, too, water enhances your enjoyment by bringing light and sparkle, reflections and movement to the patio.

Few patios are of a sufficient size to take in a pool in the real sense of the word, but constructions need not be large – some are just basins with or without a small fountain unit. Many models are available from garden centres, in a variety of sizes and styles from antique to modern. Some are very simple, say a large millstone with water bubbling through the centre, while others are complicated and have interconnecting pools. Small waterfalls can be introduced or fountains that give a constantly changing water flow. These can be illuminated to provide an attractive evening display.

Whichever style appeals to you it must fit into your patio layout. Allow plenty of space around the feature, or if space is limited put your water feature in an alcove where it can give pleasure without being a nuisance.

The selection of aquatic plants ranges from simple tufts of reed to exotic and colourful water-lilies, as well as underwater plants that provide oxygen for fish and marginal plants that hug the edge of the pool. Some will have to be planted in baskets resting on the bottom of the pool and others will grow in pockets of soil round the water's edge.

The water can support fish provided the surface area and depth are sufficient. The most common are the goldfish, of which there are many different varieties. Fish can cost from a few pence to over £50 according to their breed, colour, and size. It is possible to purchase a balanced package of plants, fish, and water snails for different sized pools from specialist water garden nurseries.

Various different types of pool construction are available, ranging from cheap to expensive. At the bottom end of the market there is the

One of the least expensive ways of constructing a pool. A hollow is dug at the chosen site and lined with plastic sheeting. Heavy stones are used to anchor the edges of the plastic as the water is poured in. The weight of the water stretches the plastic and forces it to take up the contours of the hollow.

inexpensive plastic sheet that lines a hollow dug into the ground. Ordinary polythene has a life expectancy of only a few years, but better plastics – such as PVC – are available which are less affected by sunlight. Some even have a reinforcement of nylon and carry a 10-year guarantee.

The best material for a pool liner is butyl rubber – it is even used for reservoirs! It is very tough, rotproof, easily repaired if it should be pierced accidentally, and available in any size. It usually carries a 15-year guarantee although it could last for as long as 50 years.

Liners allow you to create a pool in whatever size and shape you wish, from a small formal pool to a large, irregular lake. The pre-formed plastic and glass-fibre pools, on the other hand, come in set sizes and shapes. The hole for these must be excavated to fine limits to prevent distortion when the pool is filled with water. There are some heavy-duty models that will provide years of good service.

The most expensive type of pool is the concrete one that needs plywood shuttering into which the wet concrete is poured and held until it has dried and set. This is labour-intensive but provides a solid structure which can be any shape or style you wish. The main problem is pouring in the concrete in one go to prevent joins that can leak. If leaks do appear the pool must be drained, the crack repaired and the pool painted with a waterproofing paint.

Concrete pools should last for many years provided they have been constructed correctly with good materials, and reinforced to prevent cracking. In practice, they tend to leak after a few years of exposure to severe frosts.

Remember to 'cure' new concrete pools before adding fish or plants, by painting on a special preparation available from water garden nurseries and some garden centres.

To increase the pleasure and use of the pool there are pumps that will power fountains and waterfalls, and lights that can be used for underwater lighting or for floating on the surface. All these items need electrical power, which must be installed by a qualified electrician if you are planning to run mains-voltage equipment outdoors. Some systems utilize transformers that step down the current to 12 or 24 volts, which is perfectly safe and should not cause any installation problems.

CARE OF PATIO AND CONTAINER PLANTS

Patio and container gardening is not difficult, but it is unnatural for the plants. Often they have to grow in a volume of soil or compost that gives them only a fraction of their normal root-run, and keeping them supplied with nutrients and moisture is always a problem.

Even where plants are grown in raised beds on the patio, or in areas between the paving, their sheltered position often means roots are drier than they would be in the open garden.

To help offset these handicaps, it makes sense to give plants the best possible start with well-prepared compost or soil. As ordinary garden soil rarely gives good results in small containers, such as windowboxes and hanging baskets, it is better to use a good compost. In large containers, and in flat or raised patio beds, where compost would be too expensive to use, improving the soil is the best alternative.

SOIL FOR PATIOS

Soil is a mixture of fine particles of rock or stone, with decayed vegetation – called humus – to bind it together. It is a home to millions of micro-organisms, most beneficial but some harmful. The humus-coated particles and the spaces between them act as a reservoir of nutrients and moisture. The size of the soil particles and the spaces between them largely dictate the structure of the soil. Soil can be categorized roughly as 'heavy' (clay), 'medium' (loam), or 'light' (sandy). It is not difficult to decide which type of soil you have to work with . . . which is the first step to improving it.

Clay soils have very small air spaces between very fine particles, and this results in a sticky soil through which little air can percolate. In winter a clay soil is heavy with moisture and in summer it bakes hard, the surface cracking open as it shrinks. To improve this type of soil it is advisable to add sharp sand (really quite large grains of rock) and plenty of humus in the form of compost, manure, peat, pulverized bark and other bulky organic materials. These should help to open up the soil, allowing better drainage, and air to reach the lower levels – encouraging plants to develop better root systems. In winter the soil will be less sticky and in

summer there should be less cracking on the surface. Of course this will not happen in a couple of days, but by constantly adding and feeding the soil it will improve over the years.

Sandy soils have large grains of stone often with little humus, which makes them light and easy to work. However rain will drain away rapidly from sandy soils and wash any goodness out of it. Sandy soils also dry out quickly in summer and are often acid. Sand is quick to germinate seeds as they warm up quickly, but the plants are poor in quality as they lack moisture and nutrients. To improve a sandy soil and encourage moisture retention, dig in plenty of organic matter, farmyard manure or garden compost. Liming will reduce the acidity of the soil so that it can support a wider range of plants (but use a soil-testing kit first to be sure that it really needs it).

Loamy soils come midway between the previous two and are the nearest to ideal for most plants. If you are blessed with this soil all you need to do is to keep it in good condition, free from weeds, and to replace the nutrients that are taken out by the plants by adding manure and fertilizers.

In some areas, particularly on soil overlying natural chalk or limestone, the soil may be very alkaline – which is fine for the plants that are naturally adapted to this, but will cause many other plants to make poor, sickly growth. If you suspect your soil may be too alkaline (or too acid) check it with a soil-testing kit or a meter.

To improve the moisture-retentiveness of any soil, you can add peat, and mulch well during spring and summer, using peat, pulverized tree bark or garden compost.

Soil at the base of south-facing brick or stone walls will soon face drought conditions when a dry period occurs. To prevent the wall from absorbing moisture from this soil it is necessary to dig the soil out along the wall to a depth of 45 cm (1½ feet), exposing the wall. This is then painted with a bitumen paint and the soil replaced when the paint has dried, adding a heavy quantity of peat or compost to the soil as it is put back. This should improve the moisture level provided it is well-watered initially.

MATCHING SOILS TO PLANTS

Plants vary considerably in their soil requirements. Bog plants need a high level of moisture, while some alpines are happy in near drought conditions; campanulas enjoy a high chalk or lime content, which may kill some summer-flowering heathers, camellias, rhododendrons, and magnolias. By changing the soil it is possible to provide the correct conditions for the plant. Relatively few need a special soil. The main problem is to achieve the correct acidity or alkalinity of the soil. You can check this by using a simple soil-testing kit or meter that will give you the answer in terms of a pH factor number: 7 is neutral, above 7 is alkaline, while below 7 is acid. As the figures increase or decrease so the soil is becoming more alkaline or acid. By adding lime to the soil the pH level is increased, making it more suitable for lime-loving plants; if acid peat or flowers of sulphur are added, the soil will become more acid. It will need to be rechecked every two or three years and re-balanced.

Alpines, rockery plants, and some herbs thrive in a poor soil as long as the drainage is good. This type of soil can be simulated by mixing in a quantity of stone chippings, either limestone (for lime-loving plants) or granite (for lime-haters). The surface should be covered with a layer of chips to keep the stem base dry and to deter slugs. By growing those herbs that need a dry sunny position in a poor, well-drained soil, you will find that the aroma of the herbs becomes stronger and so fewer leaves are needed to flavour food.

PLANTING MIXES FOR CONTAINERS

Ordinary garden soil is often full of weed seeds and potential diseases and pests, and it is quite likely to be deficient in certain nutrients. Although strong, vigorous plants can usually cope with such soil, the tender ones grown in small containers are likely to succumb to at least one of these hazards. It is far better to give a good start to plants by using compost that has been specially prepared with balanced foods, sterilized to kill weed seeds and unwanted pests and diseases, and has a good structure that holds moisture while still being free-draining and allowing air to penetrate.

There are many potting composts to choose from, and both loam-based and peat-based types have their uses. The best-known soil-based composts are those made to the John Innes formula. If properly prepared from good loam these are good, but quality does vary. Soil-less composts on the other hand, can be controlled far more accurately and the quality within a particular brand is likely to be the same whether you buy the compost in Scotland or in Cornwall.

A box filled with moist soil can be a considerable weight, and with windowboxes and some containers this could be a problem. The disadvantage of light-weight peat-based composts is that they do not provide much stability for tallish plants exposed to wind. You can improve this by mixing your own compost of one part peat-based compost, one part washed river sand (not soft builders' sand), and one part expanded clay granules of the type used for

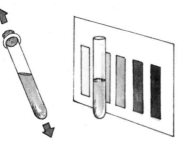

A simple soil testing kit enables you to determine whether the pH of your soil is acidic or alkaline – important to know when choosing which plants to grow.

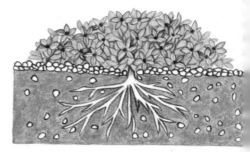

For alpine plants, mixing stone chips into the soil helps to improve drainage. A layer of chips spread on the surface of the soil acts as a mulch and deters slugs.

hydroculture and on greenhouse benching.

It is very important that all containers have good drainage. Sufficient holes should be drilled in the base to allow surplus water to drain away freely. The base of the container should be covered with a good layer of crocks or pieces of stone, brick, tile, or pottery. Some experts spread a 2.5 cm (1 inch) layer of peat over the crocks to prevent the soil being washed down and clogging the drainage holes, but in time this too will break down and filter into the crock layer. A far better method is to use a piece of capillary matting. This acts as a filter to prevent soil silting up the crocks, and also absorbs and holds moisture.

Peat can be spread on top of the matting to act as an additional reservoir of moisture, and then the container can be topped up with the compost. This should be pressed down lightly, leaving the rim of the container standing proud by at least 2.5 cm (1 inch) which will allow a mulch of peat or a layer of stones to be spread over the surface to stop moisture from evaporating too quickly. In this way a good foundation for your plants is ensured.

For deep containers increase the depth of crocks to allow less compost, unless plants that need a deep root-run, such as fruit trees or deep rooted shrubs, are being planted.

It is much more convenient to buy ready-mixed compost, but if you do want to make your own it is possible. The recipe for John Innes potting compost is:

7 parts sterilized loam
3 parts peat
2 parts sharp sand

All parts are by volume. These components should be mixed with the following proportions of John Innes base fertilizer (which you can buy ready-mixed from a garden centre) and ground chalk or limestone: To every four 9-litre (2-gallon) buckets add:

For John Innes No 1
20 g (¾ oz) ground limestone or chalk
120 g (4 oz) John Innes base fertilizer

For John Innes No 2
40 g (1½ oz) ground limestone or chalk
240 g (8 oz) John Innes base fertilizer

For John Innes No 3
65 g (2¼ oz) ground limestone or chalk
350 g (12 oz) John Innes base fertilizer

Unless you can sterilize your loam properly it is best to buy ready-mixed compost. You really need a proper sterilizing unit, which is expensive to buy unless you need a lot of compost.

Mixing your own peat-based composts is not easy either. There are problems in getting the nutrient balance right, and many of the chemicals used in commercial composts are not available to amateurs. For this reason it is best to stick to one of the good proprietary composts, or kits which contain the necessary chemicals and instructions.

FEEDING

Plants need nitrogen, phosphorus and potassium for good growth. Other minerals are also necessary in smaller quantities, such as sulphur, calcium, and magnesium. Others are needed in even smaller amounts and are referred to as trace elements: these include iron, boron, copper, zinc, and molybdenum. These nutrients are present in soil, and they are gradually absorbed by the plants.

Different types of plants have different requirements – alpines need very little food, but rampant and greedy growers will require greater quantities of goodness from the soil.

A plant that is grown for its leaves is likely to require a high level of nitrogen. This is available in a variety of forms that can be processed by the plant: Nitro-chalk is suitable for plants that can tolerate lime, sulphate of ammonia can be used for other plants. If you spurn chemical compounds, make compost from grass cuttings and pea and bean roots, or fish meal, and this will supply nitrogen to the plant in a natural form.

For good root growth the plant should be supplied with phosphorus. This can take the form of superphosphate, as a chemical preparation, or for a natural product bonemeal should be used, but make sure that it has been sterilized as it can contain disease from the animal.

Flowers and seeds of a plant are improved if there is sufficient potassium in the soil. This can be increased by adding potassium sulphate (sulphate of potash) as a chemical product, or you can use fresh wood ash (old ash will have had most of the potash washed out of it by the weather).

Some plants will have sufficient food in the soil to supply their needs and only occasionally need a little extra food. Plants in containers, however, will almost always need supplementary feeding throughout the summer. Even if a good compost was used to start with the plants will gradually exhaust the food supply. Nutrients are also leached away by rain and drainage, and can become unavailable through chemical imbalances that neutralize or 'lock up' the chemicals. For all these reasons it is usually necessary to restore nutrient levels by adding fertilizers or manures.

Fertilizers are mainly – but not exclusively – man-made chemicals and can be in liquid, powder, solid, or granular form. Manures are bulky, organic natural wastes such as farmyard manure and well-rotted leaf and vegetable matter – in fact anything that is natural, bulky, and will decay into a crumbly texture.

Manures and composts can be used in spring for non-container plants. They will gradually break down and release nutrients into the soil.

With windowboxes and containers there is insufficient space to dig in a good quantity of manure or compost. Manure can be substituted for the peat in the original soil mix as it provides plenty of fibre, but as pots and containers need a continual supply of food this is best provided by fertilizers. Liquid fertilizers should preferably be reserved for use during the growing season.

WATERING
Watering should achieve a delicate balance. Too much water will wash the goodness out of the soil, too little will stunt or kill the plants.

Some plants require more water than others. Those with soft, sappy stems and thick lush leaves indicate a thirsty plant; a thin, woody stem and a dwarf stature suggests the plant can manage with less water.

When watering it is better to soak the soil thoroughly rather than sprinkle a little on the surface as this will encourage the fine roots to come up to the surface, by which time the water will have evaporated leaving the roots to dry out and die. Always use a fine rose on the watering-can or a fine spray on the hose otherwise large drops or jets will stir up the top layer of soil exposing the fine surface roots, which will then gradually dry out making the plant less stable and more susceptible to drought.

Always bear in mind the watering problem when deciding how many containers to have.

Look for the tell-tale signs of water and nutrient deficiencies and restore them quickly. A bonemeal mulch will supplement the phosphate in the soil.

Each will need watering at least once a day during the hot days of summer: a tedious task.

PLANTING
Sowing: It is preferable to sow seeds in boxes or pots, rather than directly into the final container. They will be easier to care for and you can be using the display containers for other plants while the young ones are maturing.

Fill the container almost to the top with a good seed compost. Gently firm and moisten compost before sowing the seeds. Transplant the seedlings as soon as they are large enough.

Transplanting: Seedlings should be transplanted into trays or pots of potting compost as soon as they have formed two or so true leaves (not the seed leaves) and can be handled. Tease the tiny plants out of the compost, trying not to damage their roots or leaves. Place in holes made with a small stick and gently firm the compost around them; don't leave air pockets.

Planting out: Once the seedlings are large enough, and the conditions are right outside, they can be planted out. If the plants are tender (likely to be damaged by frost), or vulnerable to drought and wind, make sure that the weather is mild enough before planting out. It is wise to bring the plants out in the open during the day and return them to a warm place at night when the temperature falls for a few days before you plant them.

Make a hole to take the root-ball of the plant and firm it in well, then water and keep the plant and soil moist.

Larger plants, such as small trees, are sometimes sold with bare roots. Make the hole large enough to accommodate the roots when spread out. Cover them with soil, and firm it down to avoid any air pockets around the roots. All plants will need regular watering until they are established.

PROTECTION

Choosing the right position is important if you want the best from your plants. Most will need to be protected against excessive heat, cold, and wind, but you should also consider individual preferences. It is a waste of time, for instance, to try to raise a sun-loving plant in deep shade.

However, we all want to try to grow plants in places where they are not ideally suited – so efforts have to be made to improve the conditions whenever possible. For moisture-loving plants a soil that dries out rapidly can be covered with a mulch of well-rotted manure or compost, which helps to hold the water in the soil. It also protects the roots from frost.

Protection from wind can be important. Wind can turn leaves brown and stunt growth, but a screen of canes or a plastic mesh can cut down the strength of the wind to acceptable levels. Plastic mesh comes in various grades that will cut down the wind in different proportions, so you can choose a mesh most likely to provide the necessary degree of protection.

Transplant seedlings by gently teasing them out of the compost with a small stick, taking care not to damage the roots or leaves.

Plants can be protected against too much heat by providing shade. This can be achieved by a permanent structure or planting, or by erecting a temporary screen to protect the plants until they are mature. Split-cane blinds and greenhouse blinds make excellent screens.

Frost is probably one of the most obvious problems for the gardener. It sometimes comes at unexpected times in late spring and early summer before tender plants have become established. Newspapers will give adequate protection during dry weather but soon become sodden in the rain. A plastic or glass cloche will give cover against a light frost, but a layer of straw or bracken can be very effective against a more severe one.

27

PESTS AND DISEASES

Pests and diseases are the bane of a gardener's life, creeping up on plants, often unseen, and perhaps infesting them beyond cure. With one or two plants to look after you can keep an eye out for trouble, but when you grow a lot of plants it becomes more difficult.

Both pests and diseases can be brought to the garden by air, in the soil, on plants, or even on seeds. Often they spread from weeds. Many pests and diseases can be controlled by chemical sprays or dusts, but do read the small print on the container to find out what restrictions there might be – whether it is safe for children and pets; whether you can pick and eat the plant the same day as treatment, and whether you have to use the chemical at a specific time of the day. Bear this in mind when using the charts on pages 30-34.

Pests can vary from birds that peck the emerging buds to slugs that thrive on young seedlings and lush growth, from aphids that cover a plant and wither it by sucking out the sap, to microscopic organisms such as gall mites and eelworms that bore into the plants. Nature will help to control many problems by providing predators and parasites – ladybirds will eat aphids; birds will eat snails, caterpillars, and leatherjackets; hedgehogs and toads will search out many unwanted insects. So by ensuring a natural balance the pests in the garden can be kept in check. Do not expect an immediate reduction in your pest population, however, as it takes time to work.

The most effective remedy for disease is hygiene; keep your tools clean, particularly secateurs, and your soil fresh and clean. After planting out seedlings they can be watered with a fungicide to reduce fungus attack.

When a plant's leaves wilt and die, turn yellow and blotchy with lighter or darker markings, or the flowers are small and fewer in number, the plant should be examined carefully for insects, both on the surface and underneath the leaves. Where there is no sign of insect attack look for mould, fine downy hair that is not part of the plant's normal structure, and see if there is any rotting tissue (black slimy areas on the stem is a sure indication of a

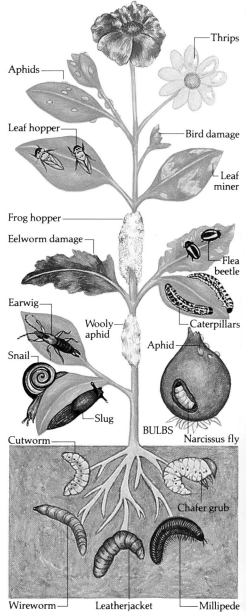

problem). If there is no sign of trouble above the ground the plant should be lifted so that the roots can be examined for swollen sections, rot, or insect attack. If there is no sign of either mould, rot or insects it could be a virus disease

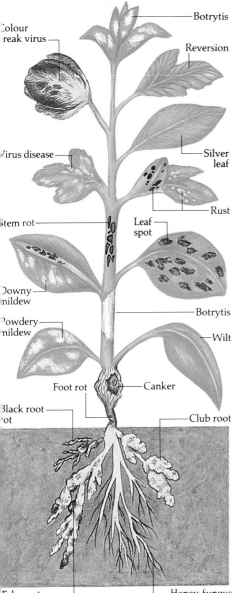

Colour
break virus

Botrytis

Reversion

Virus disease

Silver
leaf

Rust

stem rot

Leaf
spot

Downy
mildew

Powdery
mildew

Botrytis

Wilt

Foot rot

Canker

Black root
rot

Club root

Tuber rot

Honey fungus

that is attacking the plant cells. If this is the case the plant should be destroyed to prevent the virus spreading to other plants. The key to pest and disease control is to act quickly.

Just as an excess of water can damage or kill a plant so can too much chemical treatment. Full instructions for use are always given on the container, and unless these are followed precisely, the plants can suffer. For those who have a healthy dislike for chemicals in the garden there are a number of other methods of control, such as picking caterpillars off the plant by hand, using greasebands for keeping crawling insects off trees and shrubs, mothballs as a soil fumigant to discourage insects and animals underground, and netting to keep birds away from buds and fruit.

Unhealthy plants may not necessarily be the result of pest or disease attack. The soil conditions may be wrong, or excesses of heat or cold could be the cause. Look for poor growth, leaves turning yellow, or failure to flower; this could be due to a deficiency in the soil. Feed the plant with a liquid fertilizer that contains trace elements as well as the basic foods, and within a few days there should be a marked change in its appearance. Frost and sun scorch can damage leaves and stems but unless the plant is tender it should recover and regrow.

Although some plants seem prone to attacks, there are still plenty that remain trouble-free. These are normally strong plants with a good compact growth, green leaves and a healthy root-ball, and this is the type to look for when buying plants. Avoid weak and spindly looking growth, and discard plants that have been forced in a greenhouse. Instead choose plants that have been hardened off. Look for those with no damaged stems or leaves but with plenty of growth buds, and where possible buy disease-resistant varieties.

USING THE CONTROL CHARTS
Often there are several chemicals – sometimes many – that will do the same job. Those mentioned in the following charts are not all the possibilities, but are representative and give you options from which to choose. There is no substitute for reading the label carefully – sometimes there is a minimal interval between treating edible crops and eating them (it can range from days to weeks); occasionally certain plants should not be treated because they will be damaged by the chemical.

For simplicity common chemical names are used in this book – you will find them on the containers sometimes in small print.

PEST CONTROL CHART

Pest	Description	Control
Aphid (greenfly, blackfly)	The colour may vary, from green to black, but all are 1-5 mm long, soft-bodied, and with relatively long legs. They do not always have wings, in which case the plump body is conspicuous.	There are many greenfly killers, most of them very effective. Malathion is popular. Pirimicarb and permethrin are among the newer insecticides intended for aphids. There are many others, including dimethoate if you want a systematic insecticide.
Big bud mite	Only likely to affect blackcurrants. The buds become swollen – hence the common name. A tiny mite is responsible. Also known as black currant gall mite.	Chemical control is difficult. Pick off affected buds. Regular spraying with benomyl (actually a fungicide) seems to give some control.
Cabbage root fly	Although mainly a pest of cabbages, cauliflowers, and Brussels sprouts, cabbage root fly also attack wall-flowers. The plants wilt and become stunted. If lifted, the small maggots will be seen eating the roots.	Not much can be done once the plants have been attacked. As a precaution dust the soil with bromophos or diazinon when transplanting or thinning.
Capsid bug	You are most likely to see the symptoms before you see the pest. It leaves small ragged holes in the leaves, and flowers may be deformed. The insects are up to 6 mm long, but very active and are likely to drop to the ground when you look for them. The colour is usually green, but may be yellowish or brown.	A systemic insecticide such as dimethoate is particularly useful. For a non-systemic, try fenitrothion or malathion.
Caterpillars	Too well known and too diverse to warrant description. The appearance obviously depends on the species, but it makes little difference to control.	Bioresmethrin, malathion and trichlorphon will achieve control. Derris – as a spray or dust – is also effective. You can try gamma-HCH.
Codlin moth	A pest of apples. You are unlikely to notice the moths, but you will see the maggots inside the apples.	Spray with permethrin or fenitrothion just after the petals have dropped, and again three weeks later.
Earwig	Earwigs are usually about 2.5 cm (1 inch) long, brown in colour, and with 'pincers' at the end of the body. Suspect them if plants, such as dahlias (but also many others), have ragged holes torn in the leaves or petals.	Spray or dust with gamma-HCH, or use carbaryl dust. Traps should not be dismissed. An upturned flower pot on a cane, filled with straw, will attract them. You will have to empty the trap regularly and kill the earwigs.
Eelworm	Eelworms are microscopic – less than 2 mm, often smaller. There are many kinds, and symptoms vary. The ones mentioned in this book are mainly bulb and stem eelworms, affecting plants such as hyacinths and narcissi.	There is no effective cure available to amateurs. Lift and burn affected plants, and do not replant the same kind of plants in that piece of ground.

Pest	Description	Control
Eelworm (cont)	On these plants the neck of the bulb usually feels soft and if the bulb is cut across there will be dark rings of dead tissue. Growth is usually malformed or stunted.	
Flea beetle	Flea beetles make small, usually round, holes in the leaves of seedlings, and occasionally older plants. The beetles are about 3 mm long, and tend to jump.	Dust with derris or gamma-HCH.
Froghopper	It is not the froghopper insect that you are likely to notice first, but the frothy 'cuckoo spit' that appears on plants from May onwards. It protects pale coloured nymphs inside. The mature insects are up to 6 mm long, and jump when disturbed.	Malathion should give control. You may need to use a forceful spray to remove the protective froth.
Gooseberry sawfly caterpillar	Caterpillars up to 4 cm (1½) long, with black spots and head.	Spray with derris or malathion, repeating as necessary.
Leather-jackets	These greyish larvae are about 2.5 cm (1 inch) long, and are found feeding on the roots of plants, which may turn yellow and wilt, and even die.	Work bromophos or diazinon into the soil around susceptible plants.
Narcissus fly	The bulbs produce yellowish, distorted leaves, and usually fail to flower. The maggot will be found inside the rotting tissue of the bulb.	It is best to lift and burn affected bulbs.
Scab	Scab is common on apples. Greenish-brown blotches appear on the leaves; cracked, corky spots on the fruit.	Thiophanate-methyl or benomyl sprayed fortnightly from bud-burst onwards should achieve control.
Slugs and snails	Too well known to need description. There are several kinds of both slugs and snails to be found in the garden. All respond to the same treatment.	You can buy various traps, but these can have little affect on the total population. Slug pellets based on metaldehyde or methiocarb will protect plants reasonably well.
Whitefly	Small, white, rather triangular flies. Not normally a problem outdoors, but may attack the plants that you take indoors or into the greenhouse for the winter.	A systemic insecticide such as dimethoate is effective. You can spray with non-persistent insecticides such as malathion, bioresmethrin, or pyrethrum, but be prepared to repeat the application until control is achieved.

DISEASE CONTROL CHART

Disease	Description	Control
Botrytis (grey mould)	As the common name suggests, the main symptom of this disease is a grey mould – usually on dead flowers or on fruit, but it can occur on leaves or stems. A cloud of dust-like spores may be released when the affected part is moved.	Pick off any affected parts and destroy them. Then spray with benomyl or thiophanate-methyl, repeating at intervals if necessary.
Damping off	This is a disease (which can be caused by several fungi) of seedlings. The seedlings collapse where they have rotted at soil level.	Use sterilized compost as a preventative measure whenever possible. Cheshunt compound is the traditional remedy, but it is best watered into the soil before the disease has a chance to appear.
Dry rot	Dry rot can affect a number of plants with bulbs or corms, but gladioli are particularly vulnerable. The leaves turn brown and die; the corms show a number of small sunken lesions, or larger blackish areas.	Do not plant bulbs known to be infected; avoid replanting on infected ground. As a precaution soak the corms or bulbs in a solution of benomyl or thiophanate-methyl for about half an hour before planting.
Bacterial soft rot	Affects many different plants, including vegetables such as turnips and parsnips. Bulbs can become soft and slimy, with a bad smell.	There is a little to be done about the disease except to destroy affected plants, and to make sure you plant a similar crop on different ground next time.
Club-root	Although a problem of brassicas – such as cabbages and cauliflowers – it will also affect ornamentals such as wallflowers and stocks. Growth is poor and stunted, and the roots are enlarged, often with unsightly swellings.	If you are growing food crops it may be worth trying to achieve some control with root dips based on calomel or thiophanate-methyl when transplanting. For ornamental crops it is best to grow something different if you know the land is infected with club-root. Fortunately you can usually use compost for containers, so susceptible plants grown in these should be unaffected.
Leaf spot	There are several leaf spots. They may vary from small, fairly regularly shaped spots to larger, irregular blotches. The colours vary from brown to black.	Sometimes leaf spots are more disfiguring than dangerous to the plant. Spraying with benomyl or Bordeaux mixture is likely to achieve some control, but remove badly affected leaves, and be prepared to repeat the treatment.
Mildew, American gooseberry	The powdery white fungus coating on the shoots starts to appear in April. It can spread rapidly, but affects the stems more than the leaves, causing stunted growth.	Cut out badly infected shoots. Spray with benomyl or thiophanate-methyl, and be prepared to repeat the treatment.

Disease	Description	Control
Mildew, downy	The plant becomes covered with a whitish or somewhat purplish growth. Easy to confuse with powdery mildew. If you wipe the growth off with a finger, downy mildew tends to leave the plant beneath rather yellow.	Mancozeb should give some control. Not easily controlled.
Mildew, powdery	The plants – particularly leaves and shoot tips – become covered with a white, powdery-looking growth. Affected parts may become distorted.	Try a systemic fungicide, such as thiophanate-methyl, benomyl, or carbendazim. Be prepared to spray once a fortnight to achieve control. If this does not work, it may be downy mildew – in which case try mancozeb.
Peach leaf curl	This is a distinctive disease; affected plants produce distorted leaves with ugly reddish blisters.	Collect and burn affected leaves, as soon as you notice them. Spray with Bordeaux mixture after the leaves fall and again as the buds swell in late February or early March.
Rust	There are numerous rust diseases, but most produce brown or orange spots or pustules on the leaves.	Mancozeb should achieve some control, but you may have to persist with the treatment. Where rust-resistant varieties are available – as with antirrhinums, – choose these if you have had trouble in previous years.
Tomato blight	Brown blotches appear on the leaves, dark brown streaks on the stems. Fruit tends to rot.	Spray with mancozeb as a precaution in damp seasons, once the first fruit has set. Repeat at 10-day intervals.
Tulip fire	Leaves and shoots are distorted, and often withered. Flower buds usually fail to open.	Lift and destroy affected plants immediately. Do not plant suspect bulbs, and do not replant more tulips on infected land. If neighbouring tulip bulbs seem unaffected, soak them in a benomyl solution for half an hour before replanting, as a precaution.
Virus	There are many different viruses, and the symptoms vary with the disease and the plant. Suspect any plants that have distorted or stunted growth, or yellowish, mottled leaves that you cannot put down to another problem.	Virus diseases cannot be cured, and leaving the plants risks spreading the infection. Lift and burn any suspect plant.
Wilt	As the name suggests, the most common sign of wilt (there are several kinds) is wilting leaves on the plant – though they may recover at night. If the stem is cut through some distance above ground level the stem will be discoloured internally.	You can try drenching the soil with benomyl or thiophanate-methyl (made up as for a spray), and repeat the treatment. If this fails, uproot and burn the plant.

BULBS

The plants included in this chapter are grown from corms, rhizomes, and tubers, as well as true bulbs, but you can buy all of them from garden centres.

By careful selection of the different groups of 'bulbs' the patio or container gardener can obtain a colourful display of flowers all year round – late winter blooms of crocus followed by daffodils and narcissi, then hyacinths and tulips, which will run into the anemone flowering season, followed by the summer bulbs and the autumn-flowering crocus. With few gaps, that brings us back once again to the winter bulbs.

One problem with bulbs is what you do with them once they have flowered. The leaves often look untidy after flowering has finished, but you should not cut them off because they help to manufacture food that is then stored in the bulb to act as a reservoir for the following year. If you pull the leaves off too early, the bulbs will become smaller and the plants will flower less frequently.

If you want to replant the containers before the leaves have died naturally, you can lift the bulbs and replant in a convenient part of the garden to let nature take its course. Later you can lift them and store in a cool, dry place until the time comes to replant. However, if you have a garden where you can plant your old bulbs permanently, it makes sense to buy fresh bulbs each year for your container displays – at least you will be fairly sure of a good display where it matters.

You can increase your stock by separating and planting the offsets or small bulblets or cormlets that develop around the mother plant. Pick or rub off the offsets gently and plant in a separate area, known as a nursery bed, or a box of soil, until they are large enough to be planted out with mature bulbs and corms. This may take several years, and it is unwise to depend on these where your bulb display is important. Much, however, depends on the type of plant. Daffodils are relatively easy to propagate, tulips are much more unreliable.

ANEMONE*

Windflowers, as anemones are sometimes called, are ideal for patio or container cultivation. Most kinds require little attention once planted and, by successive planting, the florist's anemone (*Anemone coronaria*) can be in flower from January right through to December. However to achieve this you need to be able to offer protection and it does call for special skill.

There are two types of florist's anemone – De Caen are single, St. Brigid are double or semi-double. Both will grow up to 30 cm (1 ft) high with flowers 5 cm (2 inches) across, in white or vivid shades of red and blue.

For an early spring display, the dwarf *Anemone blanda* is most striking. It grows up to 15 cm (6 inches) high and generally has blue flowers, although white, pink and mauve forms are available. Established clumps look best. The star-like blooms can be up to 2.5 cm (1 inch) across.

General Care: Grow anemones in a good, well-drained soil with plenty of humus. The corms of *Anemone blanda* should be planted 5 cm (2 inches) deep in the autumn 10-15 cm (4-6 inches) apart. Those of the florist's anemone can also be planted in spring for a summer display.

Propagation: Anemones can be grown easily from seed or from cormlets removed and replanted in late summer.

Pests and Diseases: Slugs and snails can be troublesome as the shoots emerge, and flea beetles may also make holes in the leaves. Mottled and distorted leaves suggest a virus infection. Affected plants should be destroyed to stop the disease being transmitted to other anemones.

CROCUS*

These hardy plants are ideally suited to containers and patio borders in full sun. There are many species, but the easily obtainable Dutch hybrids have large flowers in a wide variety of colours from white through the yellows to purple, including some with stripes, coloured bases and two-tone effects. Crocus will grow up to

Pests and Diseases: Leather-jackets sometimes attack the corms. If birds are a nuisance cover the plants with a net or use strands of black cotton. Dry rot causes the corms and leaves to shrivel; lift the diseased plants and destroy. Do not replant bulbs on the same ground.

HYACINTH*

These bulbous plants bear their familiar bell-shaped flowers on a spike in spring, when they appear from a rosette of strap-like green leaves. Ideal for containers and ordinary garden use, hyacinths have a beautiful strong perfume. They come in a variety of colours, including white, yellow, pink, red, blue and purple. Growing to about 23 cm (9 inches) in height, they are compact enough for most containers.

General Care: Plant the bulbs 10 cm (4 inches) deep in the autumn in a sunny or semi-shaded site. Keep the ground free from weeds and remove dead stalks and leaves at the end of the season.

Propagation: Hyacinths can be grown from seed, but it is best to purchase bulbs produced by a specialist grower.

Pests and Diseases: Leaves and stems are sometimes attacked by eelworms, which reveal themselves as yellow stripes to the leaves. Affected plants should be destroyed and healthy bulbs moved to a fresh site. Bulbs can also be affected by rots; infected bulbs should be dug up and destroyed. Do not replant bulbs on the same ground.

12 cm (5 inches) high. There are also autumn-flowering species which will bloom from September to November (but do not confuse these with colchicums, also known as autumn crocus).

General Care: Plant the bulbs in a well-drained soil and provide some protection from wind to encourage early flowering. Do not remove heads after flowering and wait for the leaves to turn yellow before pulling them off.

Propagation: The corms produce small cormlets which can be carefully removed and grown in a separate container, where they will not be lost among other plants. They will take about two years to reach flowering size.

Crocus can also be grown from seed, but take two to four years to flower. Young plants should be grown 7.5-10 cm (3-4 inches) apart.

Rhizome iris

with a liquid fertilizer after flowering. The rhizome irises can be planted at any time, but the most satisfactory time is just after flowering.

Propagation: The bulbous irises are increased by bulb offsets. Lift the plants carefully with a fork after the foliage has died down; allow the clumps to dry for a few weeks then clean off the soil and carefully divide into single bulbs. Replant in the autumn about 10 cm (4 inches) apart.

Pests and Diseases: Most bulbs are susceptible to moulds and rot, such as bacterial soft rot. Irregularly streaked or mottled leaves may be due to viruses.

NARCISSUS* AND DAFFODIL*

The most popular of the spring-flowering bulbs, there are over 8,000 named, cultivated narcissi varieties, most of which are well-suited to windowboxes, containers and beds. They have a variety of colour that ranges from white through yellow and pink to orange; there are single and double forms with short or long trumpets, and the flowers are borne singly or in clusters on each stem. They vary in height from about 10 cm (4 inches) to about 60 cm (2 ft).

General Care: Once planted very little attention is needed. If they are in beds, keep the area weeded. Wherever the bulbs are situated, keep them well-watered in dry weather. Remove the dead flower heads so that the plant can build up strength for the following season.

IRIS*

There are two groups of iris, those with thick underground stems called rhizomes, and those that grow from bulbs. Most of the rhizome kind have sword-shaped leaves carried in a fan-like display. They grow from 25 cm (10 inches) up to about 90 cm (2½ ft).

For windowboxes, containers and small beds the smaller bulbous irises are best, as they take up less space and are more in scale with neighbouring plants. Some, such as *Iris reticulata*, will flower in the winter and spring, while others are summer-flowering. The florist's irises – Dutch, Spanish and English – are bulbous hybrids that are descended from *Iris xiphium*; they normally flower from June to July, and have a good colour range.

General Care: If grown on heavy soil, lift the bulbs after the foliage has died down and store in a dry, airy place ready for replanting in September. Bulbs can be left in the ground if grown in a lighter soil and space is not a problem. Feed

Propagation: Every three or four years the clump of bulbs should be lifted in the early summer, allowed to dry out and then split up. The bulbs can then be replanted singly, the small ones in a nursery bed where they can be weeded easily. When the bulbs are mature they can be planted out 10-20 (4-8 inches) apart.

Pests and Diseases: Narcissus fly can attack bulbs after the leaves die back. Pale stripes on the leaves and stunted plants indicate microscopic eelworms at work.

TULIP*

Tulips were brought to Holland from Turkey and other areas over 300 years ago, and began the Dutch bulb industry. The smooth, thin-skinned bulb usually produces a single flower stem normally with a deep, cup-shaped bloom. Some are double, some open out like stars, and some have petals with fringed edges. The blooms come in a wide variety of colours, from white to deep purple, including ranges of yellows, oranges, reds and mauves. If you include the small species and large-flowered kinds, their size varies from 10 cm (4 inches) to about 90 cm (3 ft).

General Care: Tulip bulbs should be planted in November, about 15 cm (6 inches) deep and not less than 10 cm (4 inches) apart. They prefer a rich soil and a reasonably sunny position. Remove the dead flower heads when the petals fall to encourage the chance of flowers the following year. Large-flowered tulips do not usually flower dependably the second year, but species and species hybrids are more reliable.

Propagation: Tulips can be grown from seed, but it is easier to use the offset bulbs found clustered round the parent bulb. Plant these at a depth of 5 cm (2 inches) in October or November; they take up to three years to reach flowering size.

Pests and Diseases: Streaked and distorted leaves suggest a virus infection. 'Scorched' specks and streaks, and distorted leaves and shoots, which occur soon after emerging, can be a serious fungal disease called tulip fire. Infected plants should be destroyed immediately. Any tulip bulbs showing signs of moulds or rots should also be destroyed.

Daffodils

ANNUALS

Plants that complete their life cycle within a year – from germinating to flowering and dying – are called annuals. They are usually easy to grow and can quickly fill a patio garden or a window-box with an enchanting display of colourful blooms.

Annuals are classified as either hardy or half-hardy. The hardy annuals can cope with the cold conditions of early spring, so they can be sown or planted out in their flowering positions even while there is a risk of frost. Half-hardy annuals are not so robust and the seeds or seedlings need to be protected from frost.

Many perennial plants are best grown as annuals – antirrhinums and impatiens are examples – either because they are not hardy or because they become less attractive with age. All these plants that are used to provide a temporary summer display are generally called bedding plants.

Most bedding plants are best raised in a greenhouse – although you can raise a few on a well-lit window ledge indoors.

As soon as the seedlings are large enough, prick them out into seed trays or small pots and keep them growing steadily in good light until ready to plant out in the open.

Before planting out, the young plants should be 'hardened off' to acclimatize them to the harsher conditions outdoors. Place the plants in a garden frame (an unheated box with a glass top would do) until they are tough enough to be planted out in the open.

Some annuals will flower for longer if you 'dead-head' them. This means cutting off the faded flower-heads to prevent seeding, which would sap the strength from the plant and result in fewer flowers.

ALYSSUM*
These hardy annuals flower throughout the summer. White is the most common flower colour, although there are pink, mauve and purple varieties. All of these are low-growing, up to 10 cm (4 inches) high, which makes them ideal for edging beds, for stone walls, and even between paving stones.

General Care: Alyssum will grow in ordinary well-drained soil in full sun. They should be dead-headed regularly with scissors to encourage further blooming.

Propagation: Sow seeds in March, transplant the seedlings into boxes and harden off before planting out, 20-30 cm (8-12 inches) apart, in their final position in April.

Alternatively the seeds can

Anthirrhinums (snapdragons)

be sown directly into the soil, thinned out, and then followed by another sowing in early May to increase the flowering season.

Pests and Diseases: Slugs are sometimes a problem with young plants. Powdery mildew is the most likely disease but is seldom a real problem.

ANTIRRHINUM*

These are the popular snapdragons. The smaller varieties can be grown in pots and borders. Some can be as low as 10 cm (4 inches). Tall varieties can grow up to 1.2 metres (4 ft). All produce spikes in a wide range of colours, in separate shades or mixtures. Some have ruffled or double flowers.

General Care: All types need a fertile well-drained soil, full sun, and regular feeding during the summer months. Pinch out the centre of the plant to make it bushy, and dead-head the flowers to prolong the flowering period.

Propagation: Sow the seeds in boxes in February or March and just cover with fine sand. Water the seeds gently, transplant and harden off before planting out at the end of May in a sunny position where they need little care. Plant intermediate varieties 45 cm (1½ ft) apart, half this distance for dwarf varieties.

Pests and Diseases: Damping-off may cause seedlings to collapse and break off at soil level. Aphids attack young plants.

Antirrhinums are particularly prone to rust, so it is worth selecting your plants from the range of rust-resistant hybrids if this has been a problem in the past.

ASTER*

The bedding plants grown as asters are really *Callistephus*, but you will nearly always find them described as 'asters'. For containers and patio beds the dwarf varieties are best. These generally grow about 15 cm (6 inches) high and are prolific, producing flowers in a wide range of vivid colours. They flower in late summer and autumn.

General Care: Grow asters in a good well-drained garden soil in a frost-free area, or provide protection from frost and cold winds. The plants should be dead-headed to encourage fresh blooms.

Asters (callistephus)

Propagation: Sow seeds in boxes in March or April, or directly into the soil from mid-April, just covering with some fine sand or compost. Protect from frost.

Pests and Diseases: Slugs may be a problem with young plants, but the major health problem is aster wilt. This turns the leaves brown and shrivelled, and the plants will die. They cannot be saved, so dig them up and burn them to prevent any spread of disease and further infection.

Powdery mildew can be disfiguring in some seasons.

CINERARIA**

Cineraria maritima, also known as *Senecio maritima*, is grown for its deeply-cut evergreen silver foliage, which provides a foil among the greener leaves of neighbouring plants. It grows to a height of 60 cm (2 ft) and has yellow flowers, 2.5 cm (1 inch) wide. The flowering period is from July to September.

General Care: Cineraria prefers a sunny position in ordinary soil. If the site is exposed, use twigs for extra support. This plant can sometimes survive winters out of doors, but is best treated as a half-hardy annual.

Propagation: Sow the seeds in trays in February or March. Transplant and harden off before planting out 30 cm (1 ft) apart at the end of May.

Pests and Diseases: Aphids may attack but cinerarias are normally disease-free.

BEGONIA SEMPERFLORENS*

This fibrous-rooted plant is perfect for patios and windowboxes. Although it can be kept indoors over the winter, it is best to buy fresh plants raised from seed each year.

There are many varieties – mainly pink or red flowers some with bronze foliage – but all are compact, seldom exceeding 15 cm (6 inches).

General Care: Plant in a sunny position, after all risk of frost has passed, and keep watered throughout the season.

Propagation: *Begonia semperflorens* is not particularly easy to raise from seed unless you have the experience and the facilities. The seed is very fine, and it needs the warmth of a propagator to germinate well. You can try raising a few plants on a warm sunny window ledge indoors. Sow in February and prick off into seed trays when they are large enough to handle.

Begonia semperflorens

Pests and Diseases: These plants are normally trouble-free, although aphids may occasionally call for action.

CALCEOLARIA**

The calceolaria suitable for bedding is *Calceolaria rugosa*. It has pouched yellow flowers, grows about 30 cm (1 ft) high, and will flower throughout the summer in a border or container.

General Care: Calceolaria like a well-drained soil with plenty of moisture, in a sunny position for good flowering, although they will tolerate partial shade.

Propagation: Sow the seeds in February or March on the surface of the compost, and shade from direct sun. They should germinate in two weeks.

Pests and Diseases: Aphids and slugs are potential hazards. Otherwise calceolaria are trouble-free.

GYPSOPHILA*

There are perennial gypsophilas for the herbaceous border and the rock garden, but the annual species usually grown is *Gypsophila elegans*. It grows about 45 cm (1½ ft) tall and bears a profusion of white or pink flowers.

General Care: These plants enjoy a sunny position in a well-drained neutral or alkaline soil. In an exposed position, it is wise to provide some protection by using twigs as an extra support.

Propagation: Sow direct into garden soil in September or March and then thin out seedlings to about 30 cm (1 ft) apart. Keep them free of weeds.

Pests and Diseases: Gypsophilas are usually trouble-free.

HELIOTROPE*

The heliotropes grown as summer bedding plants are semi-woody and form an attractive, bushy shape with clusters of tiny lavender, violet and purple flowers from June to October. They are pleasantly scented. The plant will grow up to 60 cm (2 ft) tall.

General Care: Heliotropes like a place in full sun with good, well-drained soil. It is wise to support the plants where they are exposed to high winds.

Propagation: Sow in February or March in seed trays. When the seedlings are large enough to handle, transplant into boxes. Pinch the tops out when the seedlings are 7.5 cm (3 inches) high to encourage bushiness. Harden them off before planting out 30 cm (1 ft) apart at the end of May.

Pests and Diseases: Heliotropes are generally trouble-free.

IMPATIENS*

The impatiens, popularly known as the busy Lizzie, is often regarded as a house-plant, but it also makes a superb patio and windowbox plant. Modern varieties produce compact plants with a spreading, but neat habit, and there is such a wide range of vivid colours in some of the mixtures that a bed of them is quite spectacular. In a windowbox they are most effective on their own.

There's a bonus in that these plants will grow in partial shade as well as full sun.

General Care: Do not plant impatiens out too early. They are tender and will make better plants if they can grow without a check. Do not let them become stressed through lack of water at any time.

Propagation: Unless you have a heated greenhouse or can raise a few plants indoors on a warm window ledge, it is best to buy the plants. Sow seeds in February or March and prick off into individual pots rather than boxes. It is best to raise fresh plants each year.

Pests and Diseases: Outdoors there are unlikely to be many problems, but in damp weather botrytis could set in around dead flowers.

LAVATERA**

Lavatera trimestris is a hardy annual, bushy in shape with prolific trumpet-like flowers 10 cm (4 inches) wide in deep pink and white. The flowering period is from July to September. The plants reach about 90 cm (3 feet) high, and have pale green leaves.

General Care: Lavatera prefer a sheltered, sunny position with a soil that is not over-rich. Where the plants are exposed to the wind, some cane support will be necessary.

Propagation: Sow the seed in March or April where the plants are to flower, and cover lightly with soil. In May, thin out seedlings to about 45 cm (1½ ft) apart.

Pests and Diseases: Lavatera are normally pest-free, but yellow-brown spots appearing on leaves are likely to be caused by leaf spot.

Impatiens (busy Lizzie)

Purple-flowering lobelias

LOBELIA**

The bedding lobelias are treated as half-hardy annuals and are excellent for patio borders or containers. The trailing varieties are popular for hanging baskets and for the fronts of windowboxes. The dark blue varieties are particularly popular, but pale blue can look very effective. If you want a really distinctive edging, you can buy one of the mixtures that will include pinks, reds and whites, as well as blues.
General Care: Lobelias like a rich, moist soil. They will grow in partial shade as well as full sun.
Propagation: Lobelias are easy to grow from seed. Sow the fine seeds in February or March under glass, and keep moist. Transplant in clumps of

two or three as they are too small to separate easily. Keep the seedlings relatively cool. Harden off and plant out about 10–20 cm (4–8 inches) apart in late May or early June.
Pests and Diseases: Apart from the risk of seedlings damping off, lobelias should be trouble-free.

MARIGOLD*

There are three kinds of marigold: the English pot marigold (calendula), the French marigold (*Tagetes patula*), and the African marigold (*Tagetes erecta*). The first type is hardy and will even survive the winter months unprotected, from an autumn sowing, in favourable districts. The French marigolds have small flowers on dwarf plants, while African marigolds have much larger, ball-like flowers

on taller bushier plants. There are also hybrids between the two – known as Afro-French marigolds, and these are excellent container plants, combining the best of both types.

Neither African nor French marigolds are hardy, but the pot marigold (calendula) is. If you want to grow this in containers, sow in peat pots and transplant when there is space, and be sure to grow a dwarf variety for containers.

All these marigolds have a particularly long flowering season, from early summer until the first frosts in the case of French marigolds.
General Care: All types of marigold enjoy an open, sunny place with well-drained soil. Dead-head the flowers to prolong blooming and increase flower size.
Propagation: With the tagetes sow seeds in late February or March under glass, just covering them with fine compost. Transplant the seedlings into boxes and harden off in a garden frame before planting out in their flowering positions in late May. Spacing will depend on variety – follow the advice on the seed packet.

Seeds of pot marigolds (*Calendula officinalis*) can be sown in the autumn for spring blooms if you can provide cloche protection, or sown directly into containers in March or April to provide summer flowers. If you prefer, sow in peat pots as already suggested.
Pests and Diseases: Calendulas are susceptible to mildew. African and French marigolds are prone to attack by slugs and snails when they are first planted out.

MESEMBRYANTHE-MUM*

The mesembryanthemum, used to provide a spectacular summer display from seed sown in the spring, is popularly known as the Livingstone daisy. It is a low-growing plant ideal for the edge of a border

Pot marigolds (calendulas)

or for those containers which occupy a position of full sun. The brilliantly coloured daisy-like flowers only open in bright sunlight.

The plants are only a few inches high, but can be covered with flowers up to 3.5 cm (1½ inches) across, from June to August...provided it's sunny!

General Care: Mesembryanthemums like a dry, sunny position and thrive in a light, sandy soil.

Propagation: Sow seeds in March under glass, prick out, and harden off before planting out in late May, about 23 cm (9 inches) apart.

Pests and Diseases: Mesembryanthemums are normally trouble-free, but downy mildew sometimes affects them.

NICOTIANA*

Nicotianas, commonly known as tobacco plants, range in height from 25 cm (9 inches) to about 90 cm (3 ft). They are grown for their flowers, which can be white, pink, red, maroon or green, and their delightful fragrance which perfumes the evening air from June to September. The white flowers of *Nicotiana affinis* are heavily scented but only open at dusk, while the varieties 'Daylight' and 'Dwarf White Bedder' stay open all day. The fragrant nature of the tobacco plant makes it an ideal candidate for the windowbox if you choose a very dwarf variety.

General Care: The taller varieties may require some staking to prevent them being blown over. All plants need to be dead-headed, to prolong flowering. They prefer a rich, well-drained soil in the sun.

Propagation: Plants can be raised from seed sown in a greenhouse from February to April. Plant out after hardening off, from late May onwards, when there is no significant risk of further frost.

Pests and Diseases: The young plants are quite often attacked by aphids.

PETUNIA*

Petunias have become so improved through breeding that the range of colours and forms available is very extensive. The funnel-shaped flowers are generally about 5 cm (2 inches) wide, but can be up to 12.5 cm (5 inches) across, and come in many colours, including striped blooms. The plants flower from June to the first frosts in autumn, and they are ideal for containers and windowboxes. They can also look good in hanging baskets.

Choose from Grandiflora varieties where you want large flowers, but for a massed dis-

Petunias (grandiflora variety)

play choose a Multiflora variety – it will have smaller flowers but is likely to be very prolific.

General Care: Wind and rain can damage plants, so choose weather-resistant varieties for areas that are prone to gales and storms. Grow in a sunny position, water freely, and feed regularly. Dead-head to prolong flowering.

Propagation: Sow the seeds in a heated greenhouse in March and transplant into boxes. Harden off the plants before planting out 30 cm (1 ft) apart at the end of May.

Pests and Diseases: Aphids attack young plants. Yellow-streaked and distorted leaves could be due to virus infection.

SALVIA*

Salvia splendens is the species grown for summer bedding. Although usually bright red, there are pinkish and purple shades too. Tall varieties grow to about 40 cm (16 inches), but dwarf kinds only grow to about 20 cm (8 inches).

General Care: Grow in any ordinary garden soil, preferably in a sunny position. The tips of the plants should be pinched out when they reach 7.5 cm (3 inches) high to encourage bushiness.

Propagation: Sow the seeds in trays of seed compost under glass in February or March and transplant seedlings into boxes or pots. If temperatures are too low the leaves may turn yellow and the plants become stunted. Keep protected when the weather turns chilly. Harden off salvias in a garden frame before planting out 23-38 cm (9-15 inches) apart at the end of May.

Pests and Diseases: Capsid bugs may be responsible for tattered leaves, but generally salvias are trouble-free.

STOCK*

The most popular stocks for bedding are the Ten Week type (so called because they can be brought into flower 10 weeks after sowing under glass). Normally there will always be a percentage of the less attractive single flowers, but 'selectable' types can be grown that enable you to decide at the pricking out stage which are likely to be doubles. Dwarf kinds grow to about 25 cm (10 inches), taller ones can reach 75 cm (2½ ft). The scented flowers come in a wide range of colours.

The night-scented stock, *Matthiola longipetula bicornis*, has rather dull, unexciting flowers that remain closed all day, but their lovely fragrance in the evening amply compensates for their lack of daytime interest.

General Care: Stocks enjoy full sun but will tolerate partial shade. They are best in a good garden soil that is slightly alkaline or chalky.

Propagation: Sow the seeds of Ten Week stocks under glass in February or March, then transplant into boxes and harden off before planting out in May. For later flowering the seed can be sown direct into its final position in April and the seedlings thinned out so they are about 30 cm (1 ft) apart.

Sow night-scented stocks from March to May, where they are to flower.

Pests and Diseases: Young plants can be attacked by flea beetles and aphids. Caterpillars occasionally eat the leaves of older plants. Club-root is a possibility (avoid planting stocks on infected ground).

SWEET PEA*

The container gardener will find all types of this hardy annual climber valuable. Perhaps the best varieties suited to container cultivation are the 'Knee-Hi' and 'Jet Set' groups, which grow to about 60 cm-1½ metres (2-4 ft) tall and require the minimum of support. There are also dwarf varieties that only grow 20 cm (8 inches) tall. They are robust plants producing hundreds of flowers in a wide range of single or mixed colours – from June to September. Most varieties are scented.

Sweet peas

General Care: An open, sunny position suits sweet peas best, but the plants should not be allowed to become dry, and liquid feeds are beneficial. Dead flowers should be removed to keep the peas flowering.

Propagation: Soak the seeds for 12 hours (most sweet pea seeds have a hard outer coat) before sowing in September or March under glass. Pot up the seedlings and pinch out the tips when they are 10 cm (4 inches) high. Harden off before planting out in April or May, about 15-25 cm (6-10 inches) apart.

Pests and Diseases: Young plants will probably need protecting from slugs and snails. Aphids are always a potential problem.

PERENNIALS AND BIENNIALS

A perennial plant is one that lives for several years. The term is often applied specifically to a non-woody plant that dies down in the winter and re-emerges in the spring (an herbaceous perennial), although trees and shrubs are perennials too. This chapter contains mainly herbaceous perennials, though a few shrubby plants, such as fuchsias, and 'evergreens' such as the succulent sempervivum, have been included too.

Biennials need two seasons to complete the cycle from seed to flowering, after which they die. Pansies, violas and wallflowers are amongst the most popular biennials.

Herbaceous perennials can often be increased by dividing the root with a garden fork or sharp knife. This is best done in autumn or early spring by lifting the whole root and dividing it into sections with some roots and some top growth or stalks.

AJUGA REPTANS*

This ground cover plant normally grows about 10 cm (4 inches) high, but it bears blue flowers on stems that shoot up to 30 cm (12 inches) in June and July. There are varieties with green, purple, bronze, and variegated leaves, and the plants have a spread of about 45 cm (1½ ft).

General Care: *Ajuga reptans* can be planted in any ordinary garden soil provided it is neither waterlogged nor frozen. Keep the area weeded until the plants have become established.

Propagation: The plant can be lifted and divided at any time when the soil is in an easily workable and moist state. Replant the pieces 30-45 cm (1-1½ ft) apart.

Pests and Diseases: *Ajuga reptans* is usually trouble-free.

AUBRIETA*

These low-growing, hardy plants thrive on dry walls and rocky banks. They grow to a height of 10 cm (4 inches), have a spread of up to 60 cm (2 ft), and produce a prolific display of purple to rose coloured flowers. These appear from March to June, and if the plants are trimmed right back after this flowering, they may flower again later, though more sparsely.

General Care: A sunny position is best, in ordinary garden soil. Trimming the plants after flowering will keep the shape compact.

Propagation: Aubrietas are easily grown from seed sown in February or March. Transplant to boxes, and transfer to pots when large enough to handle. Plant out in September or October.

Aubrietas can also be increased by cuttings or by division of established plants, in spring or autumn.

Pests and Diseases: Although generally pest-free, downy mildew may be seen on the undersides of the leaves.

Aubrieta

BEGONIA, TUBEROUS-ROOTED*

Begonias are particularly versatile plants and look attractive when grown in patio beds, troughs, hanging baskets, or windowboxes. The tuberous-rooted kinds used for summer bedding in sheltered places have magnificent double flowers throughout the summer. They grow 30-60 cm (1-2 ft) high and the flowers can have a diameter of 15 cm (6 inches). To make the most of hanging baskets, try the pendulous varieties. The fibrous-rooted begonias are quite different in appearance and best treated as annuals (see page 40).

Begonias can tolerate a partially shaded position and the brilliant colours of the flowers – yellow, pink, orange, and scarlet – can transform a dull corner into a blaze of colour.

General Care: Start the tubers off in boxes of moist peat in February or March. Pot on to medium sized pots of potting compost and harden off before planting out at the end of May or early June. Plant 45 cm (1½ ft) apart. A rich, moist soil is necessary, but it should also be well drained. Keep the tubers free from frost by lifting them in early October when the leaves are turning yellow, and store through winter in a box filled with dry peat and covered with newspapers.

Propagation: Old tubers can be divided into sections as they start into growth – but each piece must have a shoot. Dust the cut surfaces with sulphur powder.

Pests and Diseases: Mildew can be a problem, but begonias are generally trouble-free.

BERGENIA*

Bèrgenia

These plants form excellent ground cover as they are evergreen and low-growing, with a height of about 30 cm (12 inches) and a spread up to 60 cm (2 ft) wide. The leaves are large, glossy, and leatherlike, while the flower spikes have bell-shaped blooms that shoot up in late winter and spring. One of the advantages of bergenias is that their leaves often change to shades of red in the autumn – a time when colour is usually in short supply.

These plants grow happily in wide-rimmed flat-bottomed containers.

General Care: Bergenias will grow in any garden soil even if it is alkaline, though they appreciate a sheltered site. Remove the flower stems after blooming and place a mulch round the plant in late spring. Leave undisturbed for as long as possible.

Propagation: Divide the plant, taking some root with each piece, and replant in the autumn or March, spacing them 30-38 cm (12-15 inches) apart.

Pests and Diseases: Bergenias are normally pest-free. Sometimes the leaves show brown patches as a result of leaf spot.

CAMPANULA*

There are over 300 species and hybrids of annual and perennial campanulas known. A favourite for windowboxes and hanging baskets is *Campanula isophylla*, sometimes known as star of Bethlehem or Italian bellflower. A dwarf perennial, its blue flowers appear among the heart-shaped leaves in July or August if used outdoors. *Campanula medium*, the Canterbury bell, is a tough upright plant, growing up to 1 metre (3 ft), with hairy foliage. The bell-shaped flowers appear from May to July.

General Care: Plant in a good garden soil that is well-drained, in a sunny or partially shaded position. The taller varieties may need support in exposed positions. Feed regularly and dead-head to encourage more flowers.

Campanula isophylla is really a greenhouse plant and must be kept indoors or in a heated greenhouse through winter.

Propagation: Divide *Campanula isophylla* in spring, or take cuttings in April or May. Canterbury bells (*Campanula medium*) are biennials and must be raised from seed each year. Sow in May or June, grow on in a nursery bed, and plant in flowering positions in the autumn.

Pests and Diseases: Slugs and snails should be kept at bay. Froghoppers are an occasional problem; their frothy 'cuckoo spit', which protects them, is the most obvious sign. Orange spots on the leaves are likely to be rust disease.

DAHLIA*

Dahlias fall into two broad groups: border dahlias (usually grown for their large blooms, and raised from cuttings) and bedding dahlias (usually with smaller, often single, flowers, and raised from seed).

The large-flowered kinds can make bushy plants 1.5 metres (5 ft) high, but the small bedding dahlias usually make compact plants little more than 30 cm (1 ft) tall.

The small-growing dahlias are suitable for container cultivation, but the bigger varieties are deep rooting and difficult to grow in shallow soil.

General Care: Dahlias like an open, sunny position with a rich, moist soil. Do not plant until risk of frost has passed. Avoid over-feeding, which will cause excessive leaf growth to the detriment of flowers, but water regularly. Remove flowers as soon as they fade. Lift the tubers once the foliage has been blackened by frost, and store in a frost-proof place once they have been dried off.

Propagation: Divide the tubers in spring, making sure each piece has an 'eye', and

Campanula isophylla

plant after the last frost. If you can start them off in a greenhouse, you can take cuttings from the developing shoots instead. Bedding dahlias are best grown from seed in March; harden off the plants before planting at the end of May or early June, 30-60 cm (1-2 ft) apart.

Pests and Diseases: Aphids are often a problem. Earwigs and capsid bugs will disfigure foliage and flowers. Dahlias can also be affected by virus diseases – plants with stunted growth, mottled leaves or yellowish spots are suspect. Destroy infected plants.

DELPHINIUM*

Delphiniums are imposing plants, with tall spikes of flowers in white, blue or purple. Most varieties grow 1.2-1.8 metres (4-6 ft) high, and need staking. Try to keep to dwarf varieties for patios.

General Care: Feed and mulch in spring, water in dry periods, and stake them before they become damaged by high winds. If you cut off the dead flower spikes, the plants may flower again later in the year.

Propagation: Lift the plants in the autumn or winter and split the crown of roots into several pieces, then replant. Delphiniums can alternatively be increased from cuttings taken in April.

Pests and Diseases: If the leaves and stems appear distorted and have yellow streaks or patterns, the plant probably has a virus infection. The plant should be lifted and destroyed. A powdery deposit on the leaves is likely to be powdery mildew.

Cascading fuchsia

FESTUCA*
An ornamental grass will usually add interest to a planting scheme, and *Festuca glauca* is particularly recommended for its blue-grey leaves which provide a change of colour among the greens of other foliage. This plant grows about 23 cm (9 inches) tall. Flower heads appear in the summer, but the main attraction of festuca is its foliage, which makes an ideal edging.

General Care: Plant in a sunny position in light, well-drained soil. If you want the best from the leaves, the flower heads should be removed; if left on, they should be cut off before seeding.

Propagation: Sow seeds in a light, sandy soil in April out of doors. Transplant into tufts of

four or more when they are large enough to handle, then in the autumn plant out 15 cm (6 inches) apart in their final position. Established clumps can be divided in spring.

Pests and Diseases: Festuca is generally trouble-free.

FUCHSIA**
Fuchsias are particularly versatile plants and an ideal choice for the container gardener. They have been cross-bred to form the large variety of hardy and tender hybrids that are now available. Some fuchsias can grow over 1.8 metres (6 ft) high, while others grow less than 23 cm (9 inches) tall; some have a cascading habit that

Helianthemums

makes them perfect plants for hanging baskets and similar containers.

The distinctive flowers of most kinds hang down like a bell, with wing-like sepals, producing a characteristic appearance. Of the hundreds of named hybrids, many of the dwarf varieties are recommended for windowboxes and containers. Trailing kinds look marvellous in hanging baskets or on the edges of raised containers.

General Care: The tender varieties should be given a good moist soil and treated like a bedding plant, being put out in the open after the last frost and lifted before the first frost in the autumn. The hardy varieties should be cut back to the base and the roots protected with a layer of peat or straw during the winter. Some varieties are hardy enough to survive most winters out doors but they are unable to withstand a very harsh winter.

Fuchsias grow well in full sun or light shade and require regular watering and occasional feeding.

Propagation: You can sow seeds in March or April, and then transplant into 9 cm (3½ inch) pots when large enough to handle. Later move them to 15 cm (6 inch) pots or directly to containers of mixed plants for a summer display.

However, it is more usual to take cuttings from non flowering shoots in March. Insert 10 cm (4 inch) cuttings into a mixture of equal parts peat and sand, and keep at 16°C (61°F) until rooted.

Pests and Diseases: Aphids are a constant threat, but otherwise fuchsias are trouble-free.

HELIANTHEMUM*

Helianthemums are sun loving plants normally grown in the rock garden, but they also make good container plants. They grow up to 23 cm (9 inches) tall and spread up to 60 cm (2 ft) across. The saucer shaped flowers usually appear in June and July and are up to 2.5 cm (1 inch) wide. These flowers are commonly pink, yellow or white.

General Care: These vigorous plants can swamp neighbours, so plant with care. They thrive in ordinary garden soil with some lime; they will even grow between paving stones. Choose an open, sunny position for planting. Trim back after flowering to maintain neat shape.

Propagation: Either seeds or cuttings may be used. Sow seed in spring in trays or in the flowering position. For cuttings take a 5 cm (2 inch) non-flowering shoot with a heel of old wood in the summer, press into a pot containing a mixture of equal parts peat and sand, and place in a garden frame until rooted. Transplant to a potting compost and leave in the cold frame over winter, before planting out in the garden in April.

Pests and Diseases: Although helianthemums are normally pest-free, powdery mildew sometimes appears on these plants.

PANSY* AND VIOLA*

Although strictly perennials, pansies and violas can be treated as annuals – they will flower readily, the same summer, from a spring sowing – or as biennials. It is worth treating them as biennials for an early display. There are some winter-flowering varieties.

Most varieties reach about 23 cm (9 inches), but violas tend to have a more compact habit and smaller flowers.

General Care: Grow in a moist, well-drained soil in sun or semi-shade. Remove dead flower heads to keep the plants flowering throughout the season.

Propagation: To treat as a biennial, sow seeds in July out of doors, or in trays in a garden frame. Transplant the seedlings, placing them 10 cm (4 inches) apart. Finally replant 20-30 cm (8-12 inches) apart in their flowering positions in the autumn or early spring. Cuttings can also be taken in autumn or spring.

Pests and Diseases: Aphids may have to be controlled. These also spread virus diseases, which are likely to stunt or distort growth, and produce mottled leaves. Destroy affected plants.

Pansies

PELARGONIUM ('GERANIUM')*

The 'geraniums' generally used so effectively in containers outdoors are the zonal pelargoniums. The flower heads come mainly in bright shades of red, orange, or pink, and the plants seldom grow much more than 60 cm (2 ft) outdoors.

There are also trailing pelargoniums – ivy-leafed 'geraniums' – that make a spectacular display if planted where they can cascade effectively.

General Care: Do not plant out until risk of frost has passed. Pelargoniums love a sunny position. To make the plants bushy, pinch out the tips in spring. Keep fairly dry in winter and water moderately in summer, with occasional feeding.

Propagation: Sow seeds of suitable varieties in February, transplant into boxes and then into pots, or outside when there is no longer a risk of frost.

Alternatively, tip cuttings can be taken in March, July or September. The cuttings should be about 7.5 cm (3 inches) long, and inserted in a mixture of equal parts peat and sand. Keep shaded until they have rooted. Transplant into pots and, when the plants reach 15 cm (6 inches), pinch out the tops to make them bushy.

Pests and Diseases: Whitefly may attack pelargoniums while they are being kept in the greenhouse or indoors over winter.

POLYANTHUS* AND PRIMULA*

The primula family is diverse and includes the popular polyanthus. The polyanthus flowers, up to 4 cm (1½ inches) across, are carried in trusses on a stem about 20 cm (8 inches) tall. They are available in a wide range of colours from yellow, blue, red and pink to white. The primrose is another pretty plant, but it does not make such a bold display in the garden.

General Care: All primulas enjoy a rich, moist, fertile soil in sun or partial shade. Adding leaf mould or peat to the soil is beneficial, and regular liquid feeding during the growing months will usually help.

Propagation: A fresh supply of polyanthus is best raised from seed each year. Sow seed in trays in spring or early summer. Keep the compost moist and shade the seedlings from strong sunlight. Transplant into boxes and then set the young plants in their perma-

*Trailing pelargoniums
(ivy-leafed geraniums)*

Saxifrages

nent positions in September for flowering the following spring.

Some primulas can be divided easily after flowering and then replanted.

Pests and Diseases: Aphids and slugs are the most likely pests. Among the possible diseases, leaf spot is sometimes troublesome. Virus diseases cause stunted plants, yellow mottled and distorted leaves, and poor flowering; remove and burn affected plants to prevent the virus spreading any further.

SAXIFRAGA*

This family covers a wide range of plants; some have close-growing rosettes of leaves, some are moss-like, and others have toothed leaves. Low-growing, few are higher than 30 cm (1 ft) and most are under 10 cm (4 inches). Flowers come in a variety of colours, including pink, white and yellow, but they are rarely more than 2.5 cm (1 inch) across.

General Care: All saxifrages prefer a sunny position, and a well-drained soil with some gravel and limestone mixed in, if possible.

Propagation Most saxifrages can be divided after flowering, then replanted; otherwise non-flowering rosettes can be cut off, the lower leaves removed, and the cuttings pressed into a pot containing a mixture of equal parts sand and peat. Keep just moist until spring, then water more freely and plant out in September 20-30 cm (8-12 inches) apart to form clumps, rather than a line.

Pests and Diseases: Generally free from pests, but rust disease is a possible problem (look for brown marks) on the encrusted varieties.

SEDUM*

The sedums, or stonecrops, are succulent plants, grown for the shape and colour of the leaf as much as their star-shaped flowers.

Some varieties will grow up to 90 cm (3 ft) tall, while others only reach 1 cm (½ inch). Colours of flowers include yellow, pink, and white.

One of the largest and most spectacular is *Sedum spectabile,* which has pale green, fleshy leaves. These set off the flat, pink flower heads which appear in early autumn. The flowers are usually carried on 45 cm (1½ ft) stems and attract butterflies in large numbers whenever the sun shines.

General Care: Sedums need a well-drained, loamy soil in a sunny position. Most will withstand dry periods. After flowering, the dead stems should be left on the plants until the spring, when they can be broken off.

Propagation: Sow the seeds in a tray in March or April. Transplant the seedlings into boxes, then later into 7.5 cm (3 inch) pots, which should be kept outside until October when the young plants can be planted out.

Clumps can also be divided and replanted during the winter months.

Stem cuttings can be taken in spring and pressed into a nursery bed out of doors. Plant the larger varieties 45 cm (1½ ft) apart, the smaller ones 15 cm (6 inches) apart.

Pests and Diseases: Slugs and snails are a threat to sedum, aphids a possibility. Provided the soil is free-draining, crown and root rot should be kept to a minimum.

SEMPERVIVUM*

Sempervivums (houseleeks) are hardy and half-hardy evergreen succulents, ideal for a hot dry site. They generally grow about 2.5 cm (1 inch) high, although the tight leaf rosettes push up a leafed flowering stem which can be as tall as 20 cm (8 inches) in the summer. Sempervivums look attractive growing in shallow pans, windowboxes, troughs, and sink gardens.

General Care: Provide a sunny site with well-drained soil. To prevent the plants from spreading out too far, you can remove the outer rosettes in autumn or spring.

Propagation: Sow seeds in March in trays, and keep in a cold frame. Transplant seedlings into boxes and then plant out in position in the autumn.

Alternatively, the offsets (rosettes round the edge of the parent plant) can be detached and replanted in spring.

Pests and Diseases: They are generally pest-free apart from occasional attacks by slugs and snails. Young plants can be uprooted by birds so it is wise to cover them with a net until established.

Rust disease can be seen as orange, cup-like dimples. Lift the affected plants and burn to prevent the rust spreading.

available – yellows, oranges, reds, purples and white. They are excellent as container plants, particularly in mixed colour schemes. The dwarf types, growing only about 23-30 cm (9-12 inches) high, are especially useful for windowboxes.

General Care: These plants will thrive in a well-drained soil that is neutral or slightly alkaline. They prefer a sunny position and young plants must be protected from cold winds. The tips of the plants should be pinched out when they reach 15 cm (6 inches) in height to encourage a bushy habit.

Propagation: Sow out of doors in May or June, and transplant the seedlings to a nursery bed 15 cm (6 inches) apart in rows. In October they can be moved to their flowering positions, where they can be planted about 30 cm (1 ft) apart.

Pests and Diseases: Cabbage root fly maggots are occasionally a problem; if the plants wilt, lift one and look at the roots for signs of maggots.

Club root can be a problem on infected land – the roots will be knobbly and swollen. Do not grow wallflowers on ground known to be infected.

Wallflowers

Sedums (stonecrops)

WALLFLOWER*

Although wallflowers are hardy perennials, they are normally treated as biennials. If kept over from one flowering to the next, the plants tend to get leggy and have few flowers. Flowering in late spring and early summer, wallflowers provide a useful bridge between early bulbs and summer bedding plants. They can grow up to a height of 60 cm (2 feet), but the dwarf bedding varieties are only half this height.

A wide range of fragrant flowers in warm colours is

TREES, SHRUBS AND CLIMBERS

No design for a patio garden is complete unless attention has been given to that vital backdrop provided by trees, shrubs, and climbing plants. These give height and depth to the overall scene, offer shelter to the other plants, and privacy to the people using the patio. Most of all, they bring a welcome sense of permanency to the garden.

Because these plants are long-lived, a great deal of thought should be given to selecting the right ones. Many of the shrubs and climbers will grow happily in large pots and tubs, provided that they are looked after properly. Often the restricted root-run encourages a profusion of flowers. As a general guide, a shrub that grows to about 1-1.5 metres (3-5 ft) will require a container that is about 1 metre (3 ft) wide and 45 cm (1½ ft) deep.

When choosing a tree, bear in mind its eventual height and width, its rate of growth, and the root room it will require. For small areas it is best to select slow-growing deciduous trees or dwarf evergreens.

Some of these plants will require pruning to maintain their shape and encourage new growth.

Good ground preparation is important for trees and shrubs at any time, but if you are growing them in containers, it is even more vital. It's well worth the cost of providing a good loam-based compost, such as John Innes No. 3 potting compost. If ordinary garden soil is used for large containers, add plenty of garden compost and peat.

Above all, make sure the compost never dries out completely – something that's always a risk with containers. Trees and shrubs are as vulnerable as other plants.

You do not have to plant in containers, of course. Why not lift a paving stone and plant directly into the ground? The plant will probably be much happier.

BETULA PENDULA*

This is the common silver birch, a fast-growing tree with small leaves but graceful habit. The ordinary species grows too rapidly and too tall for a small patio, but the small weeping birch, Betula pendula 'Youngii' is well worth growing. It will grow reasonably slowly to about 4 metres (12 ft) in height, and with a spread of about 2 metres (6 ft). Catkins appear in April or May, but the silvery bark and graceful habit are the main attractions.

General Care: Birches thrive in good garden loam, but they will also tolerate a light sandy or acid soil, though on shallow chalky soil they will not reach their full height. They will grow well either in sun or partial shade. No pruning is required.

Propagation: Because Betula pendula 'Youngii' is grafted, it is best to buy a young tree from a nursery.

Pests and Diseases: Birch polypore is a bracket fungus that enters through dead wood. All dead wood should be cut out and the tree wounds treated with protective paint.

BUDDLEIA*

There are two buddleias suitable for growing on a patio, both of them very attractive deciduous shrubs. Buddleia alternifolia can be trained as a small tree with a weeping habit. The flowers are carried in long, arching sprays.

Buddleia davidii is well-known for its attraction to butterflies. These love the large, pointed sprays of white, blue, purple, or violet flowers, carried from July to October. This buddleia will grow up to 3 metres (9 ft) tall with a similar spread if left unpruned, cutting it back quite severely each spring will keep it within about 2 metres (6 ft).

General Care: Buddleias prefer to be in full sun in a good loamy soil. Prune back Buddleia davidii in March to contain size and encourage large flowers. Buddleia alternifolia should be pruned after flowering to preserve a neat shape.

Propagation: Take cuttings about 10 cm (4 inches) long with a heel of old wood in July or August. Insert the cuttings into a mixture of equal parts peat and sand, and pot up into compost once they have rooted. Stand in a garden frame until the following spring, then transplant into a nursery bed. In the autumn plant the buddleias where they are to grow.

Pests and Diseases: Normally, buddleias are relatively pest-free. If the green leaves show a pale green or yellow spotting or mottling, cucumber mosaic virus is probably responsible. The plant should be dug up and destroyed to prevent the virus spreading.

CEANOTHUS**

There are evergreen and deciduous kinds; the evergreens need some protection, such as a sheltered wall, in most of the country, but the deciduous ones are hardy. They can grow up to 3 metres (10 ft) tall. The varieties usually grown have masses of small blue flowers – in April or May, or from July to October, depending on species.

General Care: Ceanothus prefer light soil, ideally on the acid side, and a position in full sun. The tender varieties should be grown against a south- or west-facing wall. Water liberally in dry weather.

Propagation: Cuttings 10 cm (4 inches) long with a heel of old wood can be inserted in a mixture of equal parts peat and sand in July. When the cuttings have rooted, pot them up into 7.5 cm (3 inch) pots and keep in a garden frame over the winter. Transplant to their final positions in the following autumn.

Pests and Diseases: Ceanothus are sometimes attacked by scale insects. Where plants are grown on chalk chlorosis may cause the leaves to turn yellow. This disease should be treated with chelated iron and heavy mulches of acid peat.

Ceanothus

CISTUS**

These evergreen shrubs can vary from only 30 cm (1 ft) high to upright plants 2.4 metres (8 ft) tall. The plants flower prolifically from May to July, with white, pink and crimson blooms, some with contrasting markings.

General Care: A position of full sun is ideal, and they do well on dry banks and chalky soil. Cistus will tolerate wind and salt air, but they may need some protection from frost. No pruning should be carried out, apart from removing dead wood and pinching out

young growth occasionally to encourage bushiness.

Propagation: Sow seeds in March in trays, and transplant into pots when large enough to handle. Keep over winter in a garden frame and plant out in spring. Cistus can also be propagated by cuttings taken in July or August.

Pests and Diseases: Cistus are normally trouble-free but some dieback of shoots can occur as a result of frost damage. Dead wood should always be cut out.

CLEMATIS*

There are many clematis from which to choose, most of them large-flowered, but there are also some charming small-flowered species. The ones usually grown are climbers. Some will reach more than 9 metres (30 ft), but 3 metres (10 ft) is more usual for ordinary garden varieties. The large-flowered kinds have blooms up to 20 cm (8 inches) across, and there is a wide and vivid colour range.

General Care: Clematis prefer an alkaline soil in an open situation, but the base and roots should be shaded from direct sun. A cool root-run under paving is often recommended, but they are happy anywhere that their roots can be in shade and their flowers in the light.

You may have to tie in the young shoots initially, but once started they are self-supporting.

A mulch of well-rotted manure should be put over the root area in spring.

Propagation: Stem cuttings of half-ripened wood can be taken in July. Make them about 10 cm (4 inches) long with two buds at the base. Insert them in a mixture of equal parts sand and peat, and provide some bottom heat. When rooted, transplant into pots and keep in a greenhouse over the winter. In the spring harden them off and plant out in the autumn.

Pests and Diseases: Slugs and snails have an appetite for the young shoots. Aphids and earwigs can also be troublesome. The most serious disease is clematis wilt, which causes shoots to die rapidly. Cut off affected shoots and spray with benomyl or throphanate-methyl, drenching the soil too. If repeated applications fail to control it, uproot and destroy the plant.

COTONEASTER*

There are many useful cotoneasters: some evergreen, others deciduous; some ground-hugging carpeters, some large shrubs.

Two very different but useful cotoneasters for a patio are *Cotoneaster horizontalis* and *C. hybridus* 'Pendulus'.

Cotoneaster horizontalis will carpet the ground or grow upright against a wall. Either way the herringbone-like branches are attractive, and the brilliant red berries in autumn impressive.

Cotoneaster hybridus 'Pendulus' is a small weeping tree, with cascading clusters of red berries in autumn.

General Care: Cotoneasters will grow in any ordinary garden soil but need a sunny position. No annual pruning is necessary, but strong-growing plants may need pruning to keep them in shape and stop them straggling. This can be done in late winter or early spring.

Propagation: Berries of *Cotoneaster horizontalis* can be collected in September or October, the seeds removed and sown in trays. Transplant the seedlings into boxes and later into a nursery bed. After growing for two years, transplant into their final position. Cotoneasters grown from seed will not necessarily be the same variety as the parent.

Alternatively, cuttings with a heel of old wood can be taken in August, rooted in a cutting compost, and grown on in a garden frame until ready to plant out.

Low-growing cotoneasters can also be layered. Nick a branch on the underside and press into the soil; keep weighted or pegged down. New roots should grow from the wound and the new plant can be severed after about a year.

Cotoneaster hybridus 'Pendulus' is grafted, so it is best to buy a plant rather than try to propagate it yourself.

Pests and Diseases: Aphids and scale insects are the most likely pests. Fireblight makes the flowers blacken and shrivel, the branches then die back with the leaves turning brown. This is a notifiable disease and the local branch of the Ministry of Agriculture should be told of any attack – they will advise on treatment.

ERICA*

There are literally hundreds of erica (heather) varieties, which together with the closely related callunas can provide flowers for most of the year. All are evergreens, and those usually grown in small gardens vary in height from about 5 cm (2 inches) to 60 cm (2 ft). Some form excellent ground cover, requiring little attention. They have bell-shaped flowers in white, or shades of pink or purple. The leaves can vary from green to yellow, orange, or red.

Consult a specialist catalogue for details of varieties – by careful choice they will provide year-round interest.

General Care: The winter-flowering species tolerate chalk, while the rest prefer an acid, sandy or peaty soil. They will need an open, sunny situation and require some moisture during periods of drought. Cut off dead flowers after they have bloomed. Trim leggy plants to preserve a neat shape.

Propagation: Take cuttings of young side shoots up to 5 cm (2 inches) long, inserting them to a depth of a third of their lengths into pots containing a mixture of 2 parts sand to 1 part peat. Keep moist and when rooted transplant into a nursery bed. Move them to their final position when they reach 7.5 cm (3 inches) tall.

Pests and Diseases: Ericas are normally pest-free. If fungus attacks the roots and collar parts, the diseased plants should be dug up and burned and the soil replaced before growing fresh plants.

Erica arborea

EUONYMUS*

A large family of deciduous and evergreen shrubs grown for their pink berries and bright leaf colour. The deciduous varieties are hardier than their evergreen relations and are better for growing in northern areas. One of the most useful of the bushy species is *Euonymus japonicus* 'Oratus Aureus', which has yellow variegation that provides year-round interest.

General Care: The young plants should be kept moist until established, and fed with a general fertilizer in spring and summer. Euonymus grows in most soils, but plant in an open situation, particularly the variegated varieties, to ensure good leaf colour.

Propagation: Take 10 cm (4 inch) cuttings with a heel of old wood and insert them into a cutting compost. Place in a garden frame to allow them to root. The following spring the young plants should be transplanted into nursery beds for two years, and then planted out in their final positions.

Pests and Diseases: Aphids and scale insects are possible pests. The diseases to watch out for are leaf spot and powdery mildew.

JUNIPERUS*

Junipers are evergreen conifers that vary in size from the prostrate varieties of 30 cm (1 ft) high, such as *Juniperus sabina*, through dwarf forms, such as *Juniperus communis*, to shrubs and trees that can reach up to over 7.5 metres (25 ft). The colour of the foliage varies from yellow, through green to blue and grey. Some, such as the variety *Juniperus virginiana* 'Skyrocket', are pencil-shaped and add height to a patio garden, without taking up much ground space.

Select juniper varieties according to the suitability of their growing characteristics for your garden.

General Care: Junipers will grow in ordinary garden soil that is well-drained. No annual pruning is required, except to trim the shape of prostrate varieties.

Propagation: Ripe seeds from the cones can be sown in the autumn and kept in a garden frame. Transplant the seedlings into a nursery bed and allow to grow for up to two years before planting out in their final positions. Coloured and named forms should be propagated from cuttings in the autumn. Take 10 cm (4 inch) cuttings with a heel of old wood and set in a cutting compost in a garden frame. Once rooted they can be treated as seedlings.

Pests and Diseases: Scale insects can attack junipers. Rust disease may leave brown or black spots on the foliage.

Lavandula and santolinas (front)

LAVANDULA*

Lavender is a hardy, aromatic evergreen shrub grown for its scent and for use in sachets and *pot-pourris*. It can grow up to 1.2 metres (4 ft), but height depends on species and variety. The striking grey-green foliage sets off the blue to purple flowers that appear from June to September.

Lavender grows well in containers and raised beds.

General Care: Lavender will grow in any well-drained soil, but thrives best in full sun. Cut back the flowers as they die, and replace the plants every five or six years as they become old and woody.

Propagation: Take 10 cm (4 inch) long cuttings of non-flowering shoots in August. Insert them into a mixture of equal parts peat and sand, and keep in a garden frame over the winter. In spring they should be transplanted into their final positions.

Pests and Diseases: Froghoppers attack lavender plants, – the frothy 'cuckoo spit' being an obvious sign. Leaf spot and grey mould can also be problems occasionally.

LONICERA*

There are shrubby loniceras – some are used for hedges – but the most popular species are the climbing loniceras, the honeysuckles. Honeysuckles produce their fragrant flowers from May to October, depending on variety. They can grow up to 6 metres (20 ft), and are marvellous for covering walls. Shrubby honeysuckles grow

Loniceras (honeysuckles)

well in large containers.

General Care: Honeysuckles thrive in a deep, rich soil that will keep moist in dry periods. This can be helped by mulching the root area to reduce evaporation. Feed with a general fertilizer in spring and summer.

Propagation: Take 10 cm (4 inch) stem cuttings in the summer, and insert into a mixture of equal parts sand and peat. Keep in a garden frame over the winter, then transplant into pots before planting out in the garden the following autumn.

Pests and Diseases: Pests are unlikely, but powdery mildew, rust, and leaf spot are possible diseases.

PHILADELPHUS*

There are several good philadephus (mock orange) species suitable for the garden. A small hybrid such as 'Avalanche', which grows up to 1.5 metres (5 ft) tall is particularly suited to a patio garden. The profusion of white flowers in midsummer have a delicious orange blossom scent.

General Care: On the whole, philadelphus require little attention. In very dry weather the plants will need watering, and it is worth applying a thick mulch in April or May to help reduce moisture loss in the summer.

Prune out old shoots but leave the young wood.

Propagation: Take 10 cm (4 inch) cuttings of half-ripe wood in summer, inserting them into a mixture of equal parts peat and sand. Place in a garden frame for the winter and transplant into nursery beds the following spring. By the following October they will be ready to plant in their flowering positions.

Pests and Diseases: Although philadelphus are generally pest-free, they are sometimes the victims of disfiguring leaf spot diseases.

SANTOLINA*

These hardy evergreen dwarf shrubs are grown for their feathery, aromatic, silver-grey foliage and small yellow button-like blooms that appear in July. They grow about 60 cm (2 ft) tall.

General Care: Santolinas grow well in a sunny site with well-drained, sandy soil. Trim off the dead flower-heads to encourage new growth. In April the plant can be cut hard

back or trimmed to make a more compact shape.

Propagation: Take 7.5 cm (3 inch) cuttings of half-ripe sideshoots in summer. Press them into a cutting compost in a garden frame. In April pot up the rooted cuttings for planting out in the following autumn.

Pests and Diseases: Santolinas are normally trouble-free.

SENECIO*

For the patio, the evergreen shrubs of the senecio family are most useful. *Senecio greyi* and *Senecio laxifolius* are of particular interest as they have most attractive grey felted foliage; they are compact, growing about 1.2 metres (4 ft) high. Their delightful yellow daisy-like flowers in early summer are a bonus.

General Care: Plant in full sun in a good, well-drained soil, but mulch the root area to help conserve moisture. Cut off the dead flowers and cut back straggly growth in the spring to keep a good shape.

Propagation: Take 10 cm (4 inch) half-ripe cuttings in September and insert them in a mixture of equal parts sand and peat. Place in a garden frame for the winter, transplant into a nursery bed in spring, then plant out the following autumn in their final positions.

Pests and Diseases: Senecios are generally trouble-free.

WISTERIA*

These ever-popular and attractive climbers produce large drooping clusters of blue, violet, or white flowers in May and June. They are hardy deciduous plants and

can easily reach 4.5 metre (15 ft), although they usuall tend to spread sideways be fore this. They enjoy a rich soi The species often grown i *Wisteria sinensis*.

General Care: Plant in a rich deep soil against a warm wal in October or March. Mulc the root area in spring to hel keep the soil moist during th

ing out in the final position.

Wisteria sinensis can easily be layered by taking a stem that can touch the ground and pegging it to the soil in spring or autumn, where it will grow roots. After a year it can be severed from the main plant and moved to a new site.

Pests and Diseases: Aphids may have to be controlled. Bud drop can be caused by dry soil. If the soil is too alkaline the leaves may turn yellow as a result of the iron deficiency. This is termed chlorosis and should be treated by feeding with chelated iron and a heavy mulch of acid peat.

YUCCA*

Yuccas have a dramatic appearance with swordlike leaves, growing up to 75 cm (2½ ft). They bear bold bell-shaped creamy flowers on 1.8 metre (6 ft) stems in the summer. These useful evergreen plants provide an interesting contrast to more convention-al-looking patio components.

General Care: Yuccas are tough plants and grow in ordinary, well-drained soil in beds or tubs. They only need watering in severe drought conditions. The plants do not need pruning. The species grown in gardens are normal-ly hardy.

Propagation: Remove the rooted suckers that grow up beside the parent plant in spring. If they are large enough, plant them straight into their permanent posi-tions. If only small, the suckers should be planted in a nursery bed for a year and then moved to their flowering positions.

Pests and Diseases: Yuccas are normally trouble-free.

summer. Young plants should be fed in spring and summer to help them get established.

It is a good idea to restrict the growth of a mature plant by trimming new shoots back to two or three buds from the base in the winter, as this will encourage more flowers and less leaf growth.

Wisteria sinensis

Propagation: Take 10 cm (4 inch) cuttings with a heel of old wood in August, and root them in a cutting compost. Keep moist and provide bottom heat. When the cuttings have rooted, move them to a garden frame and then on to the nursery bed before plant-

FRUIT AND VEGETABLES

Most gardeners are surprised when they realize what a wide range of fruit and vegetables can be grown on balconies or patios, or even in windowboxes. The plants must be selected carefully, however, bearing in mind the limitations on root-run, space, light, and moisture.

FRUIT
Fruit crops are classified as top fruit (apples and cherries, for example) or soft fruits (such as strawberries, blackcurrants, and gooseberries). Both kinds can be grown to a restricted size if you buy the right varieties. In the case of top fruit such as apples, you also need to select a suitable rootstock.

VEGETABLES
With a little effort and ingenuity a small area can be used to produce a wide range of vegetables, although the quantity will obviously be limited. Almost any vegetable can be grown in a container or raised bed on a patio, but be sure to select the smaller varieties, as the root-run is obviously limited and space is at a premium. Growing bags can be particularly useful for vegetables on the patio.

APPLE*
The most popular fruit bush or tree, the apple, can be grown successfully on patios and in containers, but be sure to choose a variety that has been grafted on to a dwarfing rootstock such as M27 or M9. This will give a small plant that will be in scale with its neighbours.

There are various space-saving ways of training apple trees. They can take the form of a freestanding dwarf pyramid, but cordons and espaliers are worth considering. A cordon has a single stem grown at an oblique angle, an espalier has its horizontal branches trained to wires. Both espalier and fan-trained apples can be grown against a wall or framework of wires to form a screen.

You can also buy a 'family' tree which will have more than one variety grafted on to a single rootstock. Provided the vigour of each variety is carefully balanced, a 'family' tree is well worth considering if you only have enough space for one apple tree.

General Care: Apples grow in most well-drained soils, except those that are very alkaline. The centre of the tree should be pruned to keep it open and allow light in. The shape of the plant should also be controlled by pruning, and all dead and diseased wood should be removed. Apples need to be planted near a suitable pollinator if you want a good crop. If you buy a 'family' tree compatible varieties will have been chosen. Otherwise ask for advice when you buy them.

Propagation: Although apples can be grown from seed there is no guarantee of variety, so it is better to propagate by grafting. As this is a specialized job, and a suitable rootstock is essential, it is unwise to attempt this yourself.

Pests and Diseases: It is worth spraying with a winter tar-oil to control any pests which may remain on the plant through winter. Specific likely problems include codlin moth, aphids, capsid bugs, and scab.

BEANS, RUNNER*
The runner bean is a tender perennial but it is almost always grown as an annual. It can be grown as a climber against a wall or screen, or alternatively a 'wigwam' of canes can be made for the beans to grow up. This gives height to a patio, and the flowers are quite decorative – some are red, but most are white or pink.

General Care: Runner beans need moist, deep soil with plenty of humus. In periods of drought keep the soil moist by watering and mulching with a layer of peat or grass cuttings. Pick the pods before the seeds swell to encourage further cropping.

Propagation: Seeds can be planted outside in their permanent position after the danger of frost is passed at the end of May, or they can be sown in boxes under glass at the beginning of May for planting out at the end of the month. Plant at about 15 cm (6 inches) apart for best effect and heavy cropping.

Virus diseases cause stunted plants. To prevent a virus spreading to other plants dig up the affected plants and burn them.

BLACKCURRANT*

Blackcurrants, grown for their juicy, slightly acid fruit, are normally grown as bushes. They produce fruit on the previous year's growth. The plants can reach a height of 1.5 metres (5 ft) with a spread of 1.2 metres (4 ft) so you won't have room for many bushes on a patio! They are however self-fertile, so they can be grown as single bushes.

General Care: Most soils are suitable provided they are well-drained and moist. Mulch regularly with manure or compost, and apply a general fertilizer each spring. Prune new bushes to one bud above the ground, and on established plants cut out old wood before February to encourage young growth from the base.

Propagation: Insert 20 cm (8 inch) lengths of young shoots in open ground in October with only two buds showing above the soil. After a year transplant them to their fruiting site, allowing at least 1.5 metres (5 ft) between plants.

Pests and Diseases: Birds are one of the biggest problems as they can clear a good crop. The best deterrent is to cover the plant with a net. A tar-oil spray in the winter will deter aphids. Big bud is caused by a gall mite. If the cropping falls off it could be due to reversion virus, in which case the plant should be dug up and burnt. Leaf spot can be treated with a suitable fungicide.

Pests and Diseases: Slugs and snails can be a nuisance while the plants are becoming established. Aphids are a frequent problem throughout growth.

BLACKBERRY*

Although a native plant of the hedgerows, the blackberry is still worth a place in the garden. The wild blackberry bush is too well known to need description, but cultivated varieties have larger, more succulent berries – and some are even thornless!

General Care: A moist well-drained soil in sun or partial shade is best, but blackberry

Fan-trained apple tree

bushes will grow in a fairly poor soil. Cut out dead wood and train on a framework or up a wall to maintain a compact shape.

Propagation: In July, make a shallow hole in the ground and place the tip of a stem into it, then cover with soil or compost. By the following spring it will have grown roots and can be severed from the parent plant and moved to its final position.

Pests and Diseases: Raspberry beetle maggots and grey mould can spoil the fruit.

CHERRY*

There are two distinct kinds of cherry: the sweet and the acid. The acid cherry, 'Morello', is the best variety for the patio as it can be purchased as either a bush or as a fan-trained specimen for growing against a wall. However, it may still need a spread of 4.5 metres (15 ft) eventually. Unlike sweet cherries, a 'Morello' will grow well on a north-facing wall. It should flower profusely and produce deep red and black fruit in July and August.

General Care: Cherries will grow in most soils provided they are well-drained, but water regularly in dry weather to keep the soil moist. Each spring prune a few shoots to a growth bud on older wood to encourage fruiting growth.

Propagation: This is normally done by grafting or budding, and is best left to a professional. It is also advisable to purchase plants because these will probably have been partially trained.

Morello cherries

Pests and Diseases: Net the plant to stop birds eating the buds, and later the fruit. Aphids can also be a nuisance. Silver leaf disease is self-descriptive and is caused by a fungus. To treat diseased plants cut back stems and branches until clear untinted wood is found and then paint with a fungicidal paint.

CUCUMBER**

The long succulent fruits of the cucumber can provide an interesting feature in a patio garden. There are two main types of cucumber: the smooth-skinned greenhouse kind, that need to be grown with heat, and the prickly-skinned ridge varieties grown out of doors. For patios, ridge cucumbers are much more dependable.

General Care: Cucumbers need well-drained soil in full sun. Dig in plenty of well-rotted compost or manure and form a ridge, on top of which the seeds or plants can be placed. Pinch out the tips after six or seven leaves have formed. Keep the plants well watered.

Propagation: Seeds can be sown under glass at the beginning of May and the seedlings transplanted out of doors at the end of the month when the danger of a late frost is minimal. At the end of May seeds can be sown out of doors in their fruiting position.

Pests and Diseases: Although less of a problem outside than under glass, red spider mites can attack cucumbers. Spraying both sides of the leaves with water will help to deter them. Otherwise cucumbers should not be troubled by diseases outdoors, especially if grown in new growing bags.

FIG**

The fig is an almost hardy deciduous bush suitable for growing against a sunny wall. However, it is only likely to do well in favourable districts. The plant flowers one year and the fruit then takes two seasons to mature, but the large foliage is a bonus in the summer while you're waiting. Allow 4.5 metres (15 ft) for a fig to spread against a wall.

General Care: Figs will grow in good garden soil that has been fortified with bonemeal. Restrict the root-run by planting either in a well-like construction under the ground, or in a large 30 cm (12 inch) flower pot or container. Keep the roots trimmed as they tend to grow through the drainage holes.

Propagation: Branches can be layered by pegging them into the ground (roots should have formed after a year). Alternatively fig plants can be propagated from cuttings. However, you are unlikely to want more than one plant in your patio garden.

Pests and Diseases: Figs are normally pest-free. Coral spot or grey mould can cause the shoots to die back. In such cases cut off the diseased wood, then paint the wounds with fungicidal paint and spray with a systemic fungicide, such as benomyl or thiophanate-methyl.

GOOSEBERRY*

Gooseberries offer the first outdoor fresh fruit of the year – as early as May. Gooseberry plants can grow up to 1.5 metres (5 ft) tall, but most varieties produce bushes half this size.

General Care: A moist, well-drained good garden soil will suit most gooseberries. Plant in either full sun or partial shade. A mulch of well-rotted manure or compost should be applied in the spring to keep the moisture level high. Prune to keep the plant open; hard pruning of old bushes will improve the size of the fruit.

Propagation: Although gooseberries can be layered, it is more usual to take cuttings. These should be about 30 cm (1 ft) long, taken from young ripe wood. Insert them in open ground in the autumn after removing all but the top few buds. Allow to grow for a year and then transplant the healthy rooted cuttings in winter.

Pests and Diseases: Cover the bushes with nets to prevent bird damage. Aphids and gooseberry sawfly caterpillars

Black grapes

can be major problems. Grey mould can kill off the stems; cut out the dead wood and paint the wounds with a fungicidal paint.

American gooseberry mildew attacks both fruits, which are coated with a felt-like growth, and stems, which are soon crippled. This disease must be dealt with immediately, by spraying the bushes with a suitable fungicide.

GRAPE**

This hardy deciduous climber is normally grown for its fruit, but its decorative maple-like leaves help to make it an attractive feature. The vines should be trained against a south-facing wall or over a pergola for the best effect in a patio area. The flowers are borne in May, and the grapes ripen in October. Make sure you choose a variety suitable for growing outdoors – these tend to be more suitable for wine-making than for eating as a dessert fruit.

General Care: Grapes grow best in a rich, well-drained soil. After the first year, cut off two-thirds of the main stems in September, and repeat this every year until the vine fills the area required. There are many ways to prune and train grape vines, but this is a simple rule where you want the vine as a decorative feature. In young plants pinch out shoots when they reach 60 cm (2 ft) long; in mature plants cut back to two leaves beyond the flowers. It is beneficial to mulch with well-rotted manure or compost every year.

Propagation: Take 5 cm (2 inch) sections of ripe stems with one bud each in February and bury the cuttings horizontally, except for the buds, in containers of potting compost. When the cuttings have rooted, move to larger pots and then plant out in October.

As an alternative take 30 cm (1 ft) hardwood cuttings and

Peaches

insert into the soil in their growing positions out of doors. Make sure you propagate from a suitable outdoor variety.

Pests and Diseases: Net the plants to protect against bird attack. Botrytis causes fruit to rot and powdery mildew can attack leaves, fruit and shoots.

PEACH** AND NECTARINE**

Peaches and nectarines are usually grouped together as the differences are little more than skin deep and they are treated in the same way. The peach has a furry skin while the nectarine is smooth.

For patios use either a fan-trained specimen and grow against a south-facing wall, or a dwarfing stock bush that can be grown in a large tub. Even these are quite large bushes.

The fruit ripens from mid July to September.

General Care: Plant in a sheltered position. The early flowers need some protection against frost. A good rich garden soil that is well-drained will provide a good root-run and a generous mulching in spring with well-rotted manure or compost will help to keep the soil moist. Prune in February to maintain a good shape.

Propagation: Both peaches and nectarines can be grown from stones planted in pots. Crack the stone gently with nut-crackers to aid germination and plant it about 8-10 cm (3-4 inches) deep in a 9 cm (3½ inch) pot. Keep in a warm place. Once the seedling is growing strongly, transplant into the garden.

Pests and Diseases: Aphids may be a problem. Peach leaf curl is an important disease on both peaches and nectarines.

PEAR*

The pear is a hardy deciduous tree that flowers in spring. The fruit ripens between September and December according to the variety. A pear tree will grow from 2.4 metres (8 ft) up to 6 metres (20 ft) depending on the rootstock and method of training. For the patio it is better to keep to a cordon, fan, espalier, or dwarf pyramid.

General Care: Plant in a warm site for frost protection (the tree will be hardy but the blossom can be vulnerable). Pear trees appreciate good soil; they do not like a high lime content. Mulch with well-rotted manure or compost each spring. Little pruning will be required other than to remove dead wood and maintain the shape of trained plants.

Propagation: Pears are budded or grafted on to rootstocks, which are usually quince. This is difficult as the two are often incompatible and an intermediate compatible variety has to be inserted between the two. For this reason, propagation is best left to the professional.

Pests and Diseases: Aphids and birds are likely problems. Bullfinches will strip the buds off a tree in late winter. Canker can attack pears and should be treated by cutting off the diseased section and painting the wound with a fungicidal paint. Scab may also be a problem.

STRAWBERRY*

Strawberries are the simplest crop to grow in containers. Suitable containers include troughs, barrels, wheelbarrows, pots – almost anything goes!

Outdoors, strawberries begin to crop in June. For the patio, strawberry barrels are particularly effective. The plants can be inserted through numerous apertures into good rich soil inside the barrel. A large crop is possible in very little space.

General Care: A rich soil with plenty of well-rotted manure will give good crops. Protect the flowers from late frost if possible and plant in full sun.

Propagation: The runners sent out in late summer can be rooted and then transplanted.

Pests and Diseases: Net the plants to protect them from birds and use slug bait to control slugs. Grey mould is a serious disease that will rot the fruit. If plants tend to die, the area should be cleared, the plants burnt and fresh soil used for new ones.

TOMATO**

Although tomatoes are tender you can expect a reasonable outdoor crop in the warmer counties of Britain. You should, however, choose a variety suitable for growing outdoors, and some of the 'bush' types are particularly useful. These do not need to have their sideshoots removed and growth is naturally bushy. You can grow them in large pots on a patio, but growing bags are likely to be more successful.

Plant tomatoes out at the end of May or in early June in a warm and sheltered position. You should be able to harvest outdoor tomatoes during August and September.

General Care: Plant in a good, deep moist soil with plenty of humus, if pots or growing bags are not used. The plants will need staking unless a bush variety is grown.

Once flower trusses have set, feed regularly with a tomato fertilizer (one high in potash). Keep well watered throughout the season.

Propagation: Sow seeds under glass or indoors on a windowsill in late March or April and transplant seedlings into pots where they should stay until planting outdoors after the risk of frost has gone.

Pests and Diseases: Aphids are occasionally a problem but diseases such as blight are far more serious.

Dark sunken areas at the end of the fruit are caused by erratic watering while the fruit was setting and is not a disease.

Strawberries

HERBS

Most herbs are undemanding and easy to grow. You must, however, choose a suitable site and make sure they receive the maximum amount of sunshine during the growing season. Protect them from cold winds, which often cause more damage than low temperatures.

Herbs are not only useful plants, they are also decorative. Mixed plantings of annuals and perennials, such as parsley, chives, dill and thyme, in sunken sinks, troughs, pots, windowboxes or hanging baskets, can make most attractive displays.

BAY*

The sweet bay (*Laurus nobilis*) or bay laurel as it is sometimes called, is a hardy evergreen shrub. If left unrestricted it can reach a height of 5.4 metres (18 ft), but when grown in a container (and it makes an ideal container plant) with a restricted root-run it can be kept to below 2 metres (6 ft). The bay can be grown as a bush or standard, clipped to shape, or left free. The shiny dark leaves are used for flavouring fish or meat, and mixed with other herbs to form a bouquet garni.

General Care: Plant bay trees in any normal garden soil in a sunny and sheltered position or in a container with a good potting compost. Normally no pruning is necessary, but when a shape is required use secateurs to trim, not shears (which will cut the leaves leaving a brown unsightly edge).

Propagation: Take cuttings 10 cm (4 inches) long with a heel of old wood in August or September. Push the cuttings into a mixture of equal parts peat and sand, then stand in a cold frame. In spring pot up the rooted cuttings and in the following autumn plant them out in nursery beds where

Bay tree planted with begonias

they should grow for a year or so before planting them out in the spring.

Pests and Diseases: Scale insects are a potential problem.

CHIVES*

Chives, members of the onion family, are hardy perennials with grass-like leaves. They make compact plants up to 25 cm (10 inches) tall and carry attractive pale mauve flowers in June and July. The leaves are used fresh for flavouring savoury dishes. They are easy to grow and increase rapidly.

General Care: Chives will grow well in most well-drained garden soils and also in windowboxes and other containers provided they are not allowed to dry out. The flower-heads are best pinched off when the plant is being used as a herb. In winter the chives die back, re-emerging in the spring, when they should receive a dressing of well-rotted manure or compost. If grown in containers, use a liquid feed.

Propagation: Chives can be grown from seeds sown in spring. Thin out the seedlings to 15 cm (6 inches) apart and transplant to their final position in May. They can also be increased by lifting the clump in spring or autumn and dividing it into smaller clumps of up to ten shoots.

Pests and Diseases: Chives are normally trouble-free.

DILL*

This is a fragrant, hardy annual growing up to 90 cm (3 ft) tall with a hollow stem and fine, needle-like leaves. It has small yellow flowers from June to August. The leaves are

used to flavour vegetables and white meat, while the seeds have a stronger aniseed flavour and are used for pickling and flavouring sauces.

General Care: Dill grows well in most well-drained garden soils in a sunny position. Seeds are ready for collection at the end of the summer when they should be dried and stored in an airtight container.

Propagation: Sow seeds from March until July for a continual supply of fresh leaves, which are ready six to eight weeks from sowing. Thin the seedlings to 30 cm (1 ft) apart. Dill seeds itself and if allowed to do this will give good plants the following year.

Pests and Diseases: Dill is normally trouble-free.

Chives in flower

LEMON BALM*

This is a hardy perennial grown for its fragrant, lemon-scented green or yellow leaves. It grows to about 60 cm (2 ft) tall, with rather small, white flowers in June and July. The leaves and young shoots are used fresh for drinks and fruit salads, the dried leaves are mixed with other scented plants for pot-pourri.

General Care: Grow lemon balm in any well-drained soil in full sun. The richer the soil, the stronger the scent of the leaves. Plants with variegated leaves should be cut back in June to encourage new growth. In October cut back other varieties almost to ground level.

Propagation: Although easily grown from seed, it takes a long time to germinate. Sow seeds in their growing position at the end of April, thinning the seedlings to 30-45 cm (12-18 inches) apart. Alternatively, lift the root-ball in spring or autumn and divide into several pieces to replant.

Pests and Diseases: Lemon balm is normally trouble-free.

MINT*

The two mints most widely grown for herbal use are the common mint or spearmint and the apple or round-leaved mint. They are perennials growing up to 90 cm (3 ft) tall. The leaves are used to flavour lamb, tea, vegetables, iced drinks, and fruit salads. If mint is not grown in some kind of container, the roots can spread out of control.

General Care: Mints prefer a rich, moist soil but will grow in most soils as long as they have a sheltered shady position. Pick leaves or sprigs at any time until the plant dies down in the autumn to re-appear the following spring. Make a fresh bed every few years as the mint will drain the goodness out of the soil.

Propagation: Lift and divide the plants in spring. After they have been planted out give them plenty of water until they are established.

Pests and Diseases: Mints are normally pest-free. Mint rust causes the shoots to become swollen, distorted and covered with orange spores. Apart from using a fungicide, you may need to burn off the plant as it dies back in autumn to kill off any spores which could survive the winter.

Mint

PARSLEY**

All varieties of parsley are hardy biennials but are often treated as annuals to make the most of the young leaves. The curly leaves are used as a garnish and for flavouring salads, sauces, savoury dishes and stuffings. It grows up to 60 cm (2 ft) tall and has yellow flowers, which should be removed to keep the quality and flavour of the foliage. Parsley is a good plant for edging the herb garden and ideal for container growing.

General Care: Most well-drained soils will grow parsley, though it helps to incorporate some well-rotted manure or compost before sowing the seeds. Choose a sheltered position for planting and – to keep a supply going for the winter – protect from cold weather. The plants can be cut down in the autumn to encourage fresh growth.

Propagation: Sow the seeds out of doors between February and June. If the ground is cold it is better to sow the seeds in a seed tray and keep in gentle heat indoors or in a greenhouse until the spring when the seedlings can be hardened off and planted out 23 cm (9 inches) apart.

Pests and Diseases: If the leaves turn yellow with orange and red tints, the plant is probably being attacked by carrot root fly. A soil insecticide such as bromophos, used when sowing and thinning, should solve the problem.

A virus disease also causes reddish leaves, but in addition the plants are very stunted. Burn any infected plants to reduce the risk of the disease spreading further.

ROSEMARY*

There are several forms of this hardy evergreen shrub, with long, narrow leaves that are aromatic and used for flavouring meats, poultry and fish. The shoots are sometimes distilled to make rosemary oil.

The rosemary plant can grow 1.8 metres (6 ft) high eventually, but it is slow-growing. There is a dwarf variety, only 45 cm (1½ ft) high that is ideal for container growing. The little blue flowers grow in clusters from March intermittently through until September.

General Care: Rosemary needs a sunny position and a well-drained garden soil. Dead growth should be cut out in the spring and long stems should be trimmed back to maintain a compact shape. Old bushes can be cut back by half in April.

Propagation: Take 10 cm (4 inch) cuttings of half-ripe wood in the summer and insert in a mixture of equal parts sand and peat in a garden frame. Put rooted cuttings into pots for the winter and keep in frost-free surroundings until the end of May when they can be planted out in the open.

Alternatively, take 20 cm (8 inch) cuttings of mature shoots in the autumn and insert directly into the soil. The rooted cuttings should be ready to plant the following spring and summer.

Pests and Diseases: Rosemary is normally trouble-free.

SAGE*

The leaves of this hardy evergreen sub-shrub are grey-green and aromatic, and are excellent for flavouring meat and poultry. They are a popular ingredient in stuffings. Sage grows to about 60 cm (2 ft) and has small, soft purple flowers in June and July.

General Care: Sage will grow in any soil provided it is well-drained and in a sunny place. Trim the plants back to the old wood in April to maintain a compact, bushy shape; cut off the dead flowers in the autumn.

Propagation: Sow seeds in trays in the spring, then transplant the seedlings into boxes. Move them into their final position in September. Cuttings can be taken using 10 cm (4 inch) lengths of shoots in August. Insert into a mixture of equal parts peat and sand in a garden frame. Put the rooted cuttings into pots and then plant out in the open the following March.

Pests and Diseases: Sage is normally trouble-free.

THYME*

The thymes are hardy, aromatic evergreen shrubs, growing no more than 30 cm (1 ft) tall. Some varieties grow considerably less and make attractive ground cover. Thyme also does well in containers. The shoots and small leaves are

Thyme in flower

used for flavouring meat and savoury stuffings. The flowers are normally red-mauve and attract large numbers of bees in June.

General Care: Thyme enjoys a sunny position in most well-drained soils. Plants should be replaced after several years as they become thin and lanky. The plants can be clipped back after flowering to maintain a trim shape.

Propagation: Clumps of thyme can be lifted and divided in the spring, then replanted. Alternatively, 5 cm (2 inch) cuttings can be taken with a heel of old wood in May or June. Insert these into a mixture of equal parts sand and peat, in a garden frame. Pot up the rooted cuttings, but leave in the frame until autumn, then transplant into their final position.

Pests and Diseases: Thyme is normally trouble-free.

GUIDE TO SELECTING PATIO AND WINDOWBOX PLANTS

Before choosing plants for any situation you must make sure that you can provide the right conditions. Some plants prefer a sunny position, others prefer partial shade; some cannot tolerate a soil rich in lime, others thrive in it. The following chart provides you with the growing requirements of each plant – relevant to selecting ones for your situation. All are suitable for planting directly in soil on the patio; where containers are suitable, these are suggested.

PLANT	SOIL — Conditions Tolerated			SOIL — Moisture Level Tolerated		SUITABLE SITE		SIZE	SUITABLE CONTAINER			FLOWERING TIME
	Acid	Lime	Neutral	Moist	Fairly dry	Shade	Sun		Hanging basket	Tubs etc.	Windowbox	
	A	L	N	M	D	◗ ●	☀	SML	✓	✓	✓	
Ajuga Reptans	A	L	N	M		●		S	✓	✓	✓	June - July
Alyssum	A	L	N		D		☀	S	✓	✓	✓	June - Sept
Anemone	A	L	N	M		◗	☀	S	✓	✓	✓	Feb - Oct
Antirrhinum	A	L	N	M	D		☀	S/M	✓	✓	✓	June - Sept
Apple		L	N	M	D	◗	☀	L		✓		
Aster	A	L	N		D		☀	S/M	✓	✓	✓	July – Oct
Aubrieta		L	N		D		☀	S	✓	✓	✓	March - June
Balm, Lemon	A	L	N	M	D		☀	M	✓	✓	✓	
Bay	A	L	N		D	◗	☀	L		✓		
Beans - Runner	A	L	N	M			☀	L		✓		
Begonia	A	L	N	M		◗	☀	S/M	✓	✓	✓	June - Oct
Bergenia	A	L	N		D	◗	☀	S		✓		March - May
Betula Pendula (Birch)	A	L	N	M	D	◗	☀	L		✓		
Blackberry	A		N	M		◗	☀	L		✓		
Blackcurrant	A	L	N	M			☀	L		✓		
Buddleia	A	L	N	M	D	◗	☀	L		✓		July - Aug
Calceolaria	A	L	N	M			☀	M	✓	✓	✓	July - Aug
Campanula	A	L	N	M	D	◗	☀	S/L		✓	✓	July - Aug

PLANT	SOIL					SUITABLE SITE		SIZE	SUITABLE CONTAINER			FLOWERING TIME
	Conditions Tolerated			Moisture Level Tolerated					Hanging basket	Tubs etc.	Windowbox	
	Acid	Lime	Neutral	Moist	Fairly dry	Shade	Sun					
	A	L	N	M	D	◐●	☀	SML	⬒	⬛	▭	
Ceanothus	A	L	N		D		☀	L		⬛		April - May/ July - Oct
Cherry		L	N		D		☀	L		⬛		
Chives	A	L	N	M			☀	S	⬒	⬛	▭	
Cineraria	A	L	N	M	D		☀	M	⬒	⬛	▭	July - Sept
Cistus	A	L	N		D		☀	M/L		⬛		June - July
Clematis		L	N	M		◐	☀	L		⬛		May - June/ Sept - Oct
Cotoneaster	A	L	N	M	D	◐	☀	L		⬛		May - July
Crocus	A	L	N		D		☀	S	⬒	⬛	▭	March/ Sept - Nov
Cucumber	A	L	N	M			☀	S/M		⬛		
Daffodil	A	L	N		D	◐	☀	S/M	⬒	⬛	▭	March - May
Dahlia	A	L	N	M			☀	M	⬒	⬛	▭	July - Oct
Delphinium	A	L	N	M			☀	M/L		⬛		June - Aug
Dill	A	L	N	M	D		☀	M/L	⬒	⬛	▭	
Erica	A			M	D		☀	S/M			▭	Nov - Dec/ Jan - March/April
Euonymus	A	L	N		D	◐	☀	L		⬛		June - July
Festuca	A	L	N		D		☀	S	⬒	⬛	▭	
Fig	A	L	N		D		☀	L		⬛		
Fuchsia		L	N	M	D	◐	☀	S/L	⬒	⬛	▭	June - Oct
Gooseberry	A	L	N	M		◐	☀	M		⬛		
Grape	A	L	N		D		☀	L		⬛		
Gypsophila		L	N		D		☀	M/L		⬛		June - July
Helianthemum	A	L	N		D		☀	S		⬛	▭	June - Aug
Heliotrope	A	L	N		D		☀	S/M	⬒	⬛	▭	June - Oct

PLANT	SOIL					SUITABLE SITE		SIZE	SUITABLE CONTAINER			FLOWERING TIME
	Conditions Tolerated			Moisture Level Tolerated		Shade	Sun		Hanging basket	Tubs etc.	Window box	
	Acid	Lime	Neutral	Moist	Fairly dry							
	A	L	N	M	D	◐●	☀	SML	✓	✓	✓	
Hyacinth	A	L	N		D	◑	☀	S	✓	✓	✓	May
Impatiens	A	L	N	M		●◐	☀	S	✓	✓	✓	June - Oct
Iris	A	L	N	M	D		☀	S/M	✓	✓	✓	June - July
Juniperus	A	L	N	M	D	●◐	☀	S/L		✓	✓	
Lavatera	A	L	N		D		☀	M/L		✓		July - Sept
Lavandula (Lavender)	A	L	N		D		☀	L		✓	✓	July - Sept
Lobelia	A	L	N	M		◑		S	✓	✓	✓	May - Oct
Lonicera	A	L	N	M		◑	☀	L		✓		June - Aug
Marigold	A	L	N		D		☀	S/M	✓	✓	✓	June - Oct
Mesembryanthemum	A	L	N		D		☀	S	✓	✓	✓	June - Aug
Mint	A	L	N	M		●◐	☀	M	✓	✓	✓	
Narcissus	A	L	N		D	◑	☀	S/M	✓	✓	✓	March - May
Nectarine	A	L	N		D		☀	L		✓		
Nicotiana	A	L	N		D		☀	M	✓	✓	✓	June - Sept
Pansy	A	L	N		D	◑	☀	S	✓	✓	✓	April - Sept
Parsley	A	L	N	M			☀	S	✓	✓	✓	
Peach	A	L	N		D		☀	L		✓		
Pear	A		N	M			☀	L		✓		
Pelargonium (Geranium)	A	L	N		D		☀	S/M	✓	✓	✓	May - Sept
Petunia	A	L	N	M			☀	S/M	✓	✓	✓	June - Oct
Philadelphus	A	L	N		D	◐	☀	L		✓		June - July
Polyanthus	A	L	N	M		◑●	☀	S	✓	✓	✓	Jan - May
Primula	A	L	N	M		◑●	☀	S	✓	✓	✓	Jan - May

PLANT	SOIL					SUITABLE SITE		SIZE	SUITABLE CONTAINER			FLOWERING TIME
	Conditions Tolerated			Moisture Level Tolerated					Hanging basket	Tubs etc.	Window box	
	Acid	Lime	Neutral	Moist	Fairly dry	Shade	Sun					
	A	L	N	M	D	◑●	☼	SML	✓	✓	✓	
Rosemary	A	L	N		D		☼	M/L		✓	✓	
Sage	A	L	N		D		☼	M		✓	✓	
Salvia	A	L	N		D		☼	S/M	✓	✓	✓	July - Oct
Santolina	A	L	N		D		☼	M		✓	✓	July - Aug
Saxifraga	A	L	N		D	◑	☼	S	✓	✓	✓	May - June
Sedum	A	L	N		D		☼	S	✓	✓	✓	Aug - Oct
Sempervivum	A	L	N		D		☼	S		✓	✓	June - July
Senecio	A	L	N		D	◑	☼	S		✓		July - Aug
Stock		L	N		D	◑	☼	S/M	✓	✓	✓	July - Aug
Strawberry	A		N	M	D		☼	S	✓	✓	✓	
Sweet Pea	A	L	N	M			☼	L		✓		June - Sept
Thyme	A	L	N		D		☼	S	✓	✓	✓	June - Aug
Tomato	A	L	N	M			☼	M/L	✓	✓	✓	
Tulip	A	L	N		D	◑	☼	S/M	✓	✓	✓	April - May
Viola	A	L	N		D	◑	☼	S	✓	✓	✓	April - Sept
Wallflower		L	N		D		☼	S/M	✓	✓	✓	March - May
Wisteria	A	L	N	M	D		☼	L		✓		May - June
Yucca	A	L	N		D		☼	M		✓		July - Aug

INDEX

ACKNOWLEDGMENTS

Special photography by Neil Holmes

Illustrations by artists from The Garden Studio:
Christine Davison 10-13; Heather Dew 14-21, 24a;
Felicity Kays 24b, 25-28; Patti Pearce 6-9.

The publishers also wish to thank the following
individuals and organisations for their kind permission to
reproduce the photographs in this book:
Michael Boys/Octopus 37, 46, 47, 62-63, 67, 68, 72;
Jerry Harpur/Octopus 39, 59; Jacqui Hurst 23;
Harry Smith Horticultural Photographic Collection 69;
George Wright/Octopus 35, 36, 45, 50, 65, 66.